The Poetical Works Of Oliver Wendell Holmes
Vol. III

by

Oliver Wendell Holmes

Double 9
BOOKS

The Poetical Works Of Oliver Wendell Holmes
Vol. III
by Oliver Wendell Holmes

ISBN: 978-93-58591-42-2

Published by

DOUBLE 9 BOOKS

2/13-B, Ansari Road
Daryaganj, New Delhi – 110002
info@double9books.com
www.double9books.com
Tel. 011-40042856

This book is under public domain

ABOUT THE AUTHOR

Oliver Wendell Holmes Sr. (1809-1894) was an American physician, writer, and professor of anatomy and physiology at Harvard University. He was a prominent figure in American literature during the 19th century and is known for his contributions to both medicine and literature. Holmes wrote several novels, including "Elsie Venner," which was published in 1861. The book is considered a significant work of American literature and deals with themes such as original sin, the nature of good and evil, and the role of heredity in human behavior. The novel is set in a fictional New England town and tells the story of a young woman named Elsie Venner, who is believed to be the offspring of a union between a human and a rattlesnake. In addition to his literary works, Holmes is also known for his medical writing, particularly his essays on medical topics, which were published in several journals and collections.

CONTENTS

BUNKER-HILL BATTLE 9

AT THE "ATLANTIC" DINNER 14

"LUCY" 16

HYMN 18

A MEMORIAL TRIBUTE 19

JOSEPH WARREN, M. D. 22

OLD CAMBRIDGE 23

WELCOME TO THE NATIONS 27

A FAMILIAR LETTER 28

UNSATISFIED 31

HOW THE OLD HORSE WON THE BET 32

AN APPEAL FOR "THE OLD SOUTH" 38

THE FIRST FAN 40

TO R. B. H. 44

THE SHIP OF STATE 46

A FAMILY RECORD 47

THE IRON GATE 53

VESTIGIA QUINQUE RETRORSUM 56

MY AVIARY 61

ON THE THRESHOLD 64

TO GEORGE PEABODY 66

AT THE PAPYRUS CLUB 67

FOR WHITTIER'S SEVENTIETH BIRTHDAY 69

TWO SONNETS: HARVARD 71

THE COMING ERA 73

IN RESPONSE 75

FOR THE MOORE CENTENNIAL CELEBRATION 77

TO JAMES FREEMAN CLARKE 79

WELCOME TO THE CHICAGO COMMERCIAL CLUB 81

AMERICAN ACADEMY CENTENNIAL CELEBRATION 83

THE SCHOOL-BOY 86

THE SILENT MELODY 95

OUR HOME—OUR COUNTRY 97

POEM 99

RHYMES OF A LIFE-TIME 105

BEFORE THE CURFEW 106

OUR DEAD SINGER 111

TWO POEMS TO HARRIET BEECHER STOWE 113

A WELCOME TO DR. BENJAMIN APTHORP GOULD 116

TO FREDERICK HENRY HEDGE 118

TO JAMES RUSSELL LOWELL 120

TO JOHN GREENLEAF WHITTIER 122

PRELUDE TO A VOLUME PRINTED IN RAISED
LETTERS FOR THE BLIND 123

BOSTON TO FLORENCE 124

AT THE UNITARIAN FESTIVAL 125

POEM 126

POST-PRANDIAL 139

THE FLANEUR 141

AVE 145

KING'S CHAPEL 147

HYMN 149

HYMN. — THE WORD OF PROMISE 150

HYMN 152

ON THE DEATH OF PRESIDENT GARFIELD 153

THE GOLDEN FLOWER 156

HAIL, COLUMBIA! 158

ADDITIONAL VERSES 159

POEM 161

TO THE POETS WHO ONLY READ AND LISTEN 164

FOR THE DEDICATION OF THE NEW CITY
LIBRARY, BOSTON 165

FOR THE WINDOW IN ST. MARGARET'S IN
MEMORY OF A SON OF ARCHDEACON FARRAR 167

JAMES RUSSELL LOWELL 168

POEMS FROM OVER THE TEACUPS 170

THE PEAU DE CHAGRIN OF STATE STREET 172

CACOETHES SCRIBENDI 173

THE ROSE AND THE FERN 174

I LIKE YOU AND I LOVE YOU 175

LA MAISON D'OR 176

TOO YOUNG FOR LOVE 177

THE BROOMSTICK TRAIN; OR,
THE RETURN OF THE WITCHES 178

TARTARUS 182

AT THE TURN OF THE ROAD 183

IN VITA MINERVA 184

READINGS OVER THE TEACUPS 185

THE BANKER'S SECRET 188

VERSES FROM THE OLDEST PORTFOLIO 210

THE MEETING OF THE DRYADS 212

THE MYSTERIOUS VISITOR 215

THE TOADSTOOL 218

THE SPECTRE PIG... 219

TO A CAGED LION 223

THE STAR AND THE WATER-LILY 224

ILLUSTRATION OF A PICTURE 226

A ROMAN AQUEDUCT... 228

FROM A BACHELOR'S PRIVATE JOURNAL 229

LA GRISETTE 230

OUR YANKEE GIRLS.. 232

L'INCONNUE 233

STANZAS.. 234

LINES BY A CLERK... 235

THE PHILOSOPHER TO HIS LOVE... 237

THE POET'S LOT... 239

TO A BLANK SHEET OF PAPER 240

TO THE PORTRAIT OF "A GENTLEMAN" 242

THE BALLAD OF THE OYSTERMAN 244

A NOONTIDE LYRIC.. 245

THE HOT SEASON.. 247

A PORTRAIT 249

AN EVENING THOUGHT 250

THE WASP AND THE HORNET 251

"QUI VIVE?"... 252

BUNKER-HILL BATTLE

AND OTHER POEMS

1874-1877

GRANDMOTHER'S STORY OF BUNKER-HILL BATTLE

AS SHE SAW IT FROM THE BELFRY

'T is like stirring living embers when, at eighty, one remembers
All the achings and the quakings of "the times that tried men's souls";
When I talk of Whig and Tory, when I tell the Rebel story,
To you the words are ashes, but to me they're burning coals.

I had heard the muskets' rattle of the April running battle;
Lord Percy's hunted soldiers, I can see their red-coats still;
But a deadly chill comes o'er me, as the day looms up before me,
When a thousand men lay bleeding on the slopes of Bunker's Hill.

'T was a peaceful summer's morning, when the first thing gave us warning
Was the booming of the cannon from the river and the shore:
"Child," says grandma, "what 's the matter, what is all this noise and clatter?
Have those scalping Indian devils come to murder us once more?"

Poor old soul! my sides were shaking in the midst of all my quaking,
To hear her talk of Indians when the guns began to roar:
She had seen the burning village, and the slaughter and the pillage,
When the Mohawks killed her father with their bullets through his door.

Then I said, "Now, dear old granny, don't you fret and worry any,
For I'll soon come back and tell you whether this is work or play;
There can't be mischief in it, so I won't be gone a minute" —
For a minute then I started. I was gone the live-long day.

No time for bodice-lacing or for looking-glass grimacing;
Down my hair went as I hurried, tumbling half-way to my heels;
God forbid your ever knowing, when there's blood around her flowing,
How the lonely, helpless daughter of a quiet house-hold feels!

In the street I heard a thumping; and I knew it was the stumping
Of the Corporal, our old neighbor, on that wooden leg he wore,
With a knot of women round him,-it was lucky I had found him,
So I followed with the others, and the Corporal marched before.

They were making for the steeple,—the old soldier and his people;
The pigeons circled round us as we climbed the creaking stair.
Just across the narrow river—oh, so close it made me shiver!—
Stood a fortress on the hill-top that but yesterday was bare.

Not slow our eyes to find it; well we knew who stood behind it,
Though the earthwork hid them from us, and the stubborn walls were
dumb
Here were sister, wife, and mother, looking wild upon each other,
And their lips were white with terror as they
said, THE HOUR HAS COME!

The morning slowly wasted, not a morsel had we tasted,
And our heads were almost splitting with the cannons' deafening thrill,
When a figure tall and stately round the rampart strode sedately;
It was PRESCOTT, one since told me; he commanded on the hill.

Every woman's heart grew bigger when we saw his manly figure,
With the banyan buckled round it, standing up so straight and tall;
Like a gentleman of leisure who is strolling out for pleasure,
Through the storm of shells and cannon-shot he walked around the wall.

At eleven the streets were swarming, for the red-coats' ranks were
forming;
At noon in marching order they were moving to the piers;
How the bayonets gleamed and glistened, as we looked far down, and
listened
To the trampling and the drum-beat of the belted grenadiers!

At length the men have started, with a cheer (it seemed faint-hearted),
In their scarlet regimentals, with their knapsacks on their backs,
And the reddening, rippling water, as after a sea-fight's slaughter,
Round the barges gliding onward blushed like blood along their tracks.

So they crossed to the other border, and again they formed in order;
And the boats came back for soldiers, came for soldiers, soldiers still:
The time seemed everlasting to us women faint and fasting,—
At last they're moving, marching, marching proudly up the hill.

We can see the bright steel glancing all along the lines advancing,—
Now the front rank fires a volley,—they have thrown away their shot;

For behind their earthwork lying, all the balls above them flying,
Our people need not hurry; so they wait and answer not.

Then the Corporal, our old cripple (he would swear sometimes and tipple),
He had heard the bullets whistle (in the old French war) before,—
Calls out in words of jeering, just as if they all were hearing,—
And his wooden leg thumps fiercely on the dusty belfry floor:—

"Oh! fire away, ye villains, and earn King George's shillin's,
But ye 'll waste a ton of powder afore a 'rebel' falls;
You may bang the dirt and welcome, they're as safe as Dan'l Malcolm
Ten foot beneath the gravestone that you've splintered with your balls!"

In the hush of expectation, in the awe and trepidation
Of the dread approaching moment, we are well-nigh breathless all;
Though the rotten bars are failing on the rickety belfry railing,
We are crowding up against them like the waves against a wall.

Just a glimpse (the air is clearer), they are nearer,—nearer,—nearer,
When a flash—a curling smoke-wreath—then a crash—the steeple shakes—
The deadly truce is ended; the tempest's shroud is rended;
Like a morning mist it gathered, like a thunder-cloud it breaks!

Oh the sight our eyes discover as the blue-black smoke blows over!
The red-coats stretched in windrows as a mower rakes his hay;
Here a scarlet heap is lying, there a headlong crowd is flying
Like a billow that has broken and is shivered into spray.

Then we cried, "The troops are routed! they are beat—it can't be doubted!
God be thanked, the fight is over!"—Ah! the grim old soldier's smile!
"Tell us, tell us why you look so?" (we could hardly speak, we shook so),
"Are they beaten? Are they beaten? ARE they beaten?"—"Wait a while."

Oh the trembling and the terror! for too soon we saw our error:
They are baffled, not defeated; we have driven them back in vain;
And the columns that were scattered, round the colors that were tattered,
Toward the sullen, silent fortress turn their belted breasts again.

All at once, as we are gazing, lo the roofs of Charlestown blazing!
They have fired the harmless village; in an hour it will be down!
The Lord in heaven confound them, rain his fire and brimstone round them,
The robbing, murdering red-coats, that would burn a peaceful town!

They are marching, stern and solemn; we can see each massive column
As they near the naked earth-mound with the slanting walls so steep.
Have our soldiers got faint-hearted, and in noiseless haste departed?
Are they panic-struck and helpless? Are they palsied or asleep?

Now! the walls they're almost under! scarce a rod the foes asunder!
Not a firelock flashed against them! up the earth-work they will swarm!
But the words have scarce been spoken, when the ominous calm is broken,
And a bellowing crash has emptied all the vengeance of the storm!

So again, with murderous slaughter, pelted backwards to the water,
Fly Pigot's running heroes and the frightened braves of Howe;
And we shout, "At last they're done for, it's their barges they have run
for:
They are beaten, beaten, beaten; and the battle 's over now!"

And we looked, poor timid creatures, on the rough old soldier's
features,
Our lips afraid to question, but he knew what we would ask:
"Not sure," he said; "keep quiet,—once more, I guess, they 'll try it—
Here's damnation to the cut-throats!"—then he handed me his flask,

Saying, "Gal, you're looking shaky; have a drop of old Jamaiky;
I 'm afeard there 'll be more trouble afore the job is done";
So I took one scorching swallow; dreadful faint I felt and hollow,
Standing there from early morning when the firing was begun.

All through those hours of trial I had watched a calm clock dial,
As the hands kept creeping, creeping,—they were creeping round to four,
When the old man said, "They're forming with their bagonets fixed for
storming:
It 's the death-grip that's a coming,—they will try the works once
more."

With brazen trumpets blaring, the flames behind them glaring,
The deadly wall before them, in close array they come;
Still onward, upward toiling, like a dragon's fold uncoiling,—
Like the rattlesnake's shrill warning the reverberating drum.

Over heaps all torn and gory—shall I tell the fearful story,
How they surged above the breastwork, as a sea breaks over a deck;
How, driven, yet scarce defeated, our worn-out men retreated,
With their powder-horns all emptied, like the swimmers from a wreck?

It has all been told and painted; as for me, they say I fainted,
And the wooden-legged old Corporal stumped with me down the stair:

When I woke from dreams affrighted the evening lamps were lighted, —
On the floor a youth was lying; his bleeding breast was bare.

And I heard through all the flurry, "Send for WARREN! hurry! hurry!
Tell him here's a soldier bleeding, and he 'll come and dress his
wound!"
Ah, we knew not till the morrow told its tale of death and sorrow,
How the starlight found him stiffened on the dark and bloody ground.

Who the youth was, what his name was, where the place from which
he came
was,
Who had brought him from the battle, and had left him at our door,
He could not speak to tell us; but 't was one of our brave fellows,
As the homespun plainly showed us which the dying soldier wore.

For they all thought he was dying, as they gathered round him
crying, —
And they said, "Oh, how they'll miss him!" and, "What will his mother
do?"
Then, his eyelids just unclosing like a child's that has been dozing,
He faintly murmured, "Mother!" — and — I saw his eyes were blue.

"Why, grandma, how you 're winking!" Ah, my child, it sets me
thinking
Of a story not like this one. Well, he somehow lived along;
So we came to know each other, and I nursed him like a — mother,
Till at last he stood before me, tall, and rosy-checked, and strong.

And we sometimes walked together in the pleasant summer
weather, —
"Please to tell us what his name was?" Just your own, my little dear, —
There's his picture Copley painted: we became so well acquainted,
That — in short, that's why I 'm grandma, and you children all are here!

AT THE "ATLANTIC" DINNER

DECEMBER 15, 1874

I SUPPOSE it's myself that you're making allusion to
And bringing the sense of dismay and confusion to.
Of course some must speak,—they are always selected to,
But pray what's the reason that I am expected to?
I'm not fond of wasting my breath as those fellows do;
That want to be blowing forever as bellows do;
Their legs are uneasy, but why will you jog any
That long to stay quiet beneath the mahogany?

Why, why call me up with your battery of flatteries?
You say "He writes poetry,"—that's what the matter is
"It costs him no trouble—a pen full of ink or two
And the poem is done in the time of a wink or two;
As for thoughts—never mind—take the ones that lie uppermost,
And the rhymes used by Milton and Byron and Tupper most;
The lines come so easy! at one end he jingles 'em,
At the other with capital letters he shingles 'em,—
Why, the thing writes itself, and before he's half done with it
He hates to stop writing, he has such good fun with it!"

Ah, that is the way in which simple ones go about
And draw a fine picture of things they don't know about!
We all know a kitten, but come to a catamount
The beast is a stranger when grown up to that amount,
(A stranger we rather prefer should n't visit us,
A *felis* whose advent is far from felicitous.)
The boy who can boast that his trap has just got a mouse
Must n't draw it and write underneath "hippopotamus";
Or say unveraciously, "This is an elephant,"—
Don't think, let me beg, these examples irrelevant,—
What they mean is just this—that a thing to be painted well
Should always be something with which we're acquainted well.

You call on your victim for "things he has plenty of, —
Those copies of verses no doubt at least twenty of;
His desk is crammed full, for he always keeps writing 'em
And reading to friends as his way of delighting 'em!"
I tell you this writing of verses means business, —
It makes the brain whirl in a vortex of dizziness
You think they are scrawled in the languor of laziness—
I tell you they're squeezed by a spasm of craziness,
A fit half as bad as the staggering vertigos
That seize a poor fellow and down in the dirt he goes!

And therefore it chimes with the word's etytology
That the sons of Apollo are great on apology,
For the writing of verse is a struggle mysterious
And the gayest of rhymes is a matter that's serious.
For myself, I'm relied on by friends in extremities,
And I don't mind so much if a comfort to them it is;
'T is a pleasure to please, and the straw that can tickle us
Is a source of enjoyment though slightly ridiculous.

I am up for a—something—and since I 've begun with it,
I must give you a toast now before I have done with it.
Let me pump at my wits as they pumped the Cochituate
That moistened—it may be—the very last bit you ate:
Success to our publishers, authors and editors
To our debtors good luck,—pleasant dreams to our creditors;
May the monthly grow yearly, till all we are groping for
Has reached the fulfilment we're all of us hoping for;
Till the bore through the tunnel—it makes me let off a sigh
To think it may possibly ruin my prophecy—
Has been punned on so often 't will never provoke again
One mild adolescent to make the old joke again;
Till abstinent, all-go-to-meeting society
Has forgotten the sense of the word inebriety;
Till the work that poor Hannah and Bridget and Phillis do
The humanized, civilized female gorillas do;
Till the roughs, as we call them, grown loving and dutiful,
Shall worship the true and the pure and the beautiful,
And, preying no longer as tiger and vulture do,
All read the "Atlantic" as persons of culture do!

"LUCY"

FOR HER GOLDEN WEDDING, OCTOBER 18, 1875

"Lucy." —The old familiar name
Is now, as always, pleasant,
Its liquid melody the same
Alike in past or present;
Let others call you what they will,
I know you'll let me use it;
To me your name is Lucy still,
I cannot bear to lose it.

What visions of the past return
With Lucy's image blended!
What memories from the silent urn
Of gentle lives long ended!
What dreams of childhood's fleeting morn,
What starry aspirations,
That filled the misty days unborn
With fancy's coruscations!

Ah, Lucy, life has swiftly sped
From April to November;
The summer blossoms all are shed
That you and I remember;
But while the vanished years we share
With mingling recollections,
How all their shadowy features wear
The hue of old affections!

Love called you. He who stole your heart
Of sunshine half bereft us;
Our household's garland fell apart
The morning that you left us;

The tears of tender girlhood streamed
Through sorrow's opening sluices;
Less sweet our garden's roses seemed,
Less blue its flower-de-luces.

That old regret is turned to smiles,
That parting sigh to greeting;
I send my heart-throb fifty miles
Through every line 't is beating;
God grant you many and happy years,
Till when the last has crowned you
The dawn of endless day appears,
And heaven is shining round you!

October 11, 1875.

HYMN

FOR THE INAUGURATION OF THE STATUE OF GOVERNOR ANDREW, HINGHAM, OCTOBER 7, 1875

BEHOLD the shape our eyes have known!
It lives once more in changeless stone;
So looked in mortal face and form
Our guide through peril's deadly storm.

But hushed the beating heart we knew,
That heart so tender, brave, and true,
Firm as the rooted mountain rock,
Pure as the quarry's whitest block!

Not his beneath the blood-red star
To win the soldier's envied sear;
Unarmed he battled for the right,
In Duty's never-ending fight.

Unconquered will, unslumbering eye,
Faith such as bids the martyr die,
The prophet's glance, the master's hand
To mould the work his foresight planned,

These were his gifts; what Heaven had lent
For justice, mercy, truth, he spent,
First to avenge the traitorous blow,
And first to lift the vanquished foe.

Lo, thus he stood; in danger's strait
The pilot of the Pilgrim State!
Too large his fame for her alone, —
A nation claims him as her own!

A MEMORIAL TRIBUTE

READ AT THE MEETING HELD AT MUSIC HALL, FEBRUARY 8, 1876, IN MEMORY OF DR. SAMUEL G. HOWE

I.

LEADER of armies, Israel's God,
Thy soldier's fight is won!
Master, whose lowly path he trod,
Thy servant's work is done!

No voice is heard from Sinai's steep
Our wandering feet to guide;
From Horeb's rock no waters leap;
No Jordan's waves divide;

No prophet cleaves our western sky
On wheels of whirling fire;
No shepherds hear the song on high
Of heaven's angelic choir.

Yet here as to the patriarch's tent
God's angel comes a guest;
He comes on heaven's high errand sent,
In earth's poor raiment drest.

We see no halo round his brow
Till love its own recalls,
And, like a leaf that quits the bough,
The mortal vesture falls.

In autumn's chill declining day,
Ere winter's killing frost,
The message came; so passed away
The friend our earth has lost.

Still, Father, in thy love we trust;
Forgive us if we mourn
The saddening hour that laid in dust
His robe of flesh outworn.

II.

How long the wreck-strewn journey seems
To reach the far-off past
That woke his youth from peaceful dreams
With Freedom's trumpet-blast.

Along her classic hillsides rung
The Paynim's battle-cry,
And like a red-cross knight he sprung
For her to live or die.

No trustier service claimed the wreath
For Sparta's bravest son;
No truer soldier sleeps beneath
The mound of Marathon;

Yet not for him the warrior's grave
In front of angry foes;
To lift, to shield, to help, to save,
The holier task he chose.

He touched the eyelids of the blind,
And lo! the veil withdrawn,
As o'er the midnight of the mind
He led the light of dawn.

He asked not whence the fountains roll
No traveller's foot has found,
But mapped the desert of the soul
Untracked by sight or sound.

What prayers have reached the sapphire throne,
By silent fingers spelt,
For him who first through depths unknown
His doubtful pathway felt,

Who sought the slumbering sense that lay
Close shut with bolt and bar,
And showed awakening thought the ray
Of reason's morning star.

Where'er he moved, his shadowy form
The sightless orbs would seek,
And smiles of welcome light and warm
The lips that could not speak.

No labored line, no sculptor's art,
Such hallowed memory needs;
His tablet is the human heart,
His record loving deeds.

III.

The rest that earth denied is thine, —
Ah, is it rest? we ask,
Or, traced by knowledge more divine,
Some larger, nobler task?

Had but those boundless fields of blue
One darkened sphere like this;
But what has heaven for thee to do
In realms of perfect bliss?

No cloud to lift, no mind to clear,
No rugged path to smooth,
No struggling soul to help and cheer,
No mortal grief to soothe!

Enough; is there a world of love,
No more we ask to know;
The hand will guide thy ways above
That shaped thy task below.

JOSEPH WARREN, M. D.

TRAINED in the holy art whose lifted shield
Wards off the darts a never-slumbering foe,
By hearth and wayside lurking, waits to throw,
Oppression taught his helpful arm to wield
The slayer's weapon: on the murderous field
The fiery bolt he challenged laid him low,
Seeking its noblest victim. Even so
The charter of a nation must be sealed!
The healer's brow the hero's honors crowned,
From lowliest duty called to loftiest deed.
Living, the oak-leaf wreath his temples bound;
Dying, the conqueror's laurel was his meed,
Last on the broken ramparts' turf to bleed
Where Freedom's victory in defeat was found.

June 11, 1875.

OLD CAMBRIDGE

JULY 3, 1875

AND can it be you've found a place
Within this consecrated space,
That makes so fine a show,
For one of Rip Van Winkle's race?
And is it really so?
Who wants an old receipted bill?
Who fishes in the Frog-pond still?
Who digs last year's potato hill? —
That's what he'd like to know!

And were it any spot on earth
Save this dear home that gave him birth
Some scores of years ago,
He had not come to spoil your mirth
And chill your festive glow;
But round his baby-nest he strays,
With tearful eye the scene surveys,
His heart unchanged by changing days,
That's what he'd have you know.

Can you whose eyes not yet are dim
Live o'er the buried past with him,
And see the roses blow
When white-haired men were Joe and Jim
Untouched by winter's snow?
Or roll the years back one by one
As Judah's monarch backed the sun,
And see the century just begun? —
That's what he'd like to know!

I come, but as the swallow dips,
Just touching with her feather-tips
The shining wave below,
To sit with pleasure-murmuring lips
And listen to the flow
Of Elmwood's sparkling Hippocrene,

To tread once more my native green,
To sigh unheard, to smile unseen,—
That's what I'd have you know.

But since the common lot I've shared
(We all are sitting "unprepared,"
Like culprits in a row,
Whose heads are down, whose necks are bared
To wait the headsman's blow),
I'd like to shift my task to you,
By asking just a thing or two
About the good old times I knew,—
Here's what I want to know.

The yellow meetin' house—can you tell
Just where it stood before it fell
Prey of the vandal foe,—
Our dear old temple, loved so well,
By ruthless hands laid low?
Where, tell me, was the Deacon's pew?
Whose hair was braided in a queue?
(For there were pig-tails not a few,)—
That's what I'd like to know.

The bell—can you recall its clang?
And how the seats would slam and bang?
The voices high and low?
The basso's trump before he sang?
The viol and its bow?
Where was it old Judge Winthrop sat?
Who wore the last three-cornered hat?
Was Israel Porter lean or fat?—
That's what I'd like to know.

Tell where the market used to be
That stood beside the murdered tree?
Whose dog to church would go?
Old Marcus Reemie, who was he?
Who were the brothers Snow?
Does not your memory slightly fail
About that great September gale?—
Whereof one told a moving tale,
As Cambridge boys should know.

When Cambridge was a simple town,
Say just when Deacon William Brown

(Last door in yonder row),
For honest silver counted down,
His groceries would bestow?—
For those were days when money meant
Something that jingled as you went,—
No hybrid like the nickel cent,
I'd have you all to know,

But quarter, ninepence, pistareen,
And fourpence hapennies in between,
All metal fit to show,
Instead of rags in stagnant green,
The scum of debts we owe;
How sad to think such stuff should be
Our Wendell's cure-all recipe,—
Not Wendell H., but Wendell P.,—
The one you all must know!

I question—but you answer not—
Dear me! and have I quite forgot
How fivescore years ago,
Just on this very blessed spot,
The summer leaves below,
Before his homespun ranks arrayed
In green New England's elmbough shade
The great Virginian drew the blade
King George full soon should know!

O George the Third! you found it true
Our George was more than double you,
For nature made him so.
Not much an empire's crown can do
If brains are scant and slow,—
Ah, not like that his laurel crown
Whose presence gilded with renown
Our brave old Academic town,
As all her children know!

So here we meet with loud acclaim
To tell mankind that here he came,
With hearts that throb and glow;
Ours is a portion of his fame
Our trumpets needs must blow!
On yonder hill the Lion fell,
But here was chipped the eagle's shell,—
That little hatchet did it well,

As all the world shall know!

WELCOME TO THE NATIONS

PHILADELPHIA, JULY 4, 1876

BRIGHT on the banners of lily and rose
Lo! the last sun of our century sets!
Wreathe the black cannon that scowled on our foes,
All but her friendships the nation forgets
All but her friends and their welcome forgets!
These are around her; but where are her foes?
Lo, while the sun of her century sets,
Peace with her garlands of lily and rose!

Welcome! a shout like the war trumpet's swell
Wakes the wild echoes that slumber around
Welcome! it quivers from Liberty's bell;
Welcome! the walls of her temple resound!
Hark! the gray walls of her temple resound
Fade the far voices o'er hillside and dell;
Welcome! still whisper the echoes around;
Welcome I still trembles on Liberty's bell!

Thrones of the continents! isles of the sea
Yours are the garlands of peace we entwine;
Welcome, once more, to the land of the free,
Shadowed alike by the pahn and the pine;
Softly they murmur, the palm and the pine,
"Hushed is our strife, in the land of the free";
Over your children their branches entwine,
Thrones of the continents! isles of the sea!

A FAMILIAR LETTER

TO SEVERAL CORRESPONDENTS

YES, write, if you want to, there's nothing like trying;
Who knows what a treasure your casket may hold?
I'll show you that rhyming's as easy as lying,
If you'll listen to me while the art I unfold.

Here's a book full of words; one can choose as he fancies,
As a painter his tint, as a workman his tool;
Just think! all the poems and plays and romances
Were drawn out of this, like the fish from a pool!

You can wander at will through its syllabled mazes,
And take all you want,—not a copper they cost,—
What is there to hinder your picking out phrases
For an epic as clever as "Paradise Lost"?

Don't mind if the index of sense is at zero,
Use words that run smoothly, whatever they mean;
Leander and Lilian and Lillibullero
Are much the same thing in the rhyming machine.

There are words so delicious their sweetness will smother
That boarding-school flavor of which we 're afraid,—
There is "lush" is a good one, and "swirl" another,—
Put both in one stanza, its fortune is made.

With musical murmurs and rhythmical closes
You can cheat us of smiles when you've nothing to tell;
You hand us a nosegay of milliner's roses,
And we cry with delight, "Oh, how sweet they do smell!"

Perhaps you will answer all needful conditions
For winning the laurels to which you aspire,
By docking the tails of the two prepositions
I' the style o' the bards you so greatly admire.

As for subjects of verse, they are only too plenty
For ringing the changes on metrical chimes;

A maiden, a moonbeam, a lover of twenty
Have filled that great basket with bushels of rhymes.

Let me show you a picture—'tis far from irrelevant—
By a famous old hand in the arts of design;
'T is only a photographed sketch of an elephant,—
The name of the draughtsman was Rembrandt of Rhine.

How easy! no troublesome colors to lay on,
It can't have fatigued him,—no, not in the least,—
A dash here and there with a hap-hazard crayon,
And there stands the wrinkled-skinned, baggy-limbed beast.

Just so with your verse,—'t is as easy as sketching,—
You—can reel off a song without knitting your brow,
As lightly as Rembrandt a drawing or etching;
It is nothing at all, if you only know how.

Well; imagine you've printed your volume of verses:
Your forehead is wreathed with the garland of fame,
Your poems the eloquent school-boy rehearses,
Her album the school-girl presents for your name;

Each morning the post brings you autograph letters;
You'll answer them promptly,—an hour is n't much
For the honor of sharing a page with your betters,
With magistrates, members of Congress, and such.

Of course you're delighted to serve the committees
That come with requests from the country all round,
You would grace the occasion with poems and ditties
When they've got a new schoolhouse, or poor-house, or pound.

With a hymn for the saints and a song for the sinners,
You go and are welcome wherever you please;
You're a privileged guest at all manner of dinners,
You've a seat on the platform among the grandees.

At length your mere presence becomes a sensation,
Your cup of enjoyment is filled to its brim
With the pleasure Horatian of digitmonstration,
As the whisper runs round of "That's he!" or "That Is him!"

But remember, O dealer in phrases sonorous,
So daintily chosen, so tunefully matched,
Though you soar with the wings of the cherubim o'er us,
The ovum was human from which you were hatched.

No will of your own with its puny compulsion
Can summon the spirit that quickens the lyre;
It comes, if at all, like the Sibyl's convulsion
And touches the brain with a finger of fire.

So perhaps, after all, it's as well to be quiet,
If you've nothing you think is worth saying in prose,
As to furnish a meal of their cannibal diet
To the critics, by publishing, as you propose.

But it's all of no use, and I 'm sorry I've written, —
I shall see your thin volume some day on my shelf;
For the rhyming tarantula surely has bitten,
And music must cure you, so pipe it yourself.

UNSATISFIED

"ONLY a housemaid!" She looked from the kitchen, —
Neat was the kitchen and tidy was she;
There at her window a sempstress sat stitching;
"Were I a sempstress, how happy I'd be!"

"Only a Queen!" She looked over the waters, —
Fair was her kingdom and mighty was she;
There sat an Empress, with Queens for her daughters;
"Were I an Empress, how happy I'd be!"

Still the old frailty they all of them trip in!
Eve in her daughters is ever the same;
Give her all Eden, she sighs for a pippin;
Give her an Empire, she pines for a name!

May 8, 1876.

HOW THE OLD HORSE WON THE BET

DEDICATED BY A CONTRIBUTOR TO THE COLLEGIAN,
1830, TO THE EDITORS OF THE HARVARD ADVOCATE, 1876.

'T WAS on the famous trotting-ground,
The betting men were gathered round
From far and near; the "cracks" were there
Whose deeds the sporting prints declare
The swift g. m., Old Hiram's nag,
The fleet s. h., Dan Pfeiffer's brag,
With these a third—and who is he
That stands beside his fast b. g.?
Budd Doble, whose catarrhal name
So fills the nasal trump of fame.
There too stood many a noted steed
Of Messenger and Morgan breed;
Green horses also, not a few;
Unknown as yet what they could do;
And all the hacks that know so well
The scourgings of the Sunday swell.

Blue are the skies of opening day;
The bordering turf is green with May;
The sunshine's golden gleam is thrown
On sorrel, chestnut, bay, and roan;
The horses paw and prance and neigh,
Fillies and colts like kittens play,
And dance and toss their rippled manes
Shining and soft as silken skeins;
Wagons and gigs are ranged about,
And fashion flaunts her gay turn-out;
Here stands—each youthful Jehu's dream
The jointed tandem, ticklish team!
And there in ampler breadth expand
The splendors of the four-in-hand;
On faultless ties and glossy tiles

The lovely bonnets beam their smiles;
(The style's the man, so books avow;
The style's the woman, anyhow);
From flounces frothed with creamy lace
Peeps out the pug-dog's smutty face,
Or spaniel rolls his liquid eye,
Or stares the wiry pet of Skye,—
O woman, in your hours of ease
So shy with us, so free with these!

"Come on! I 'll bet you two to one
I 'll make him do it!" "Will you? Done!"

What was it who was bound to do?
I did not hear and can't tell you,—
Pray listen till my story's through.

Scarce noticed, back behind the rest,
By cart and wagon rudely prest,
The parson's lean and bony bay
Stood harnessed in his one-horse shay—
Lent to his sexton for the day;
(A funeral—so the sexton said;
His mother's uncle's wife was dead.)

Like Lazarus bid to Dives' feast,
So looked the poor forlorn old beast;
His coat was rough, his tail was bare,
The gray was sprinkled in his hair;
Sportsmen and jockeys knew him not,
And yet they say he once could trot
Among the fleetest of the town,
Till something cracked and broke him down,—
The steed's, the statesman's, common lot!
"And are we then so soon forgot?"
Ah me! I doubt if one of you
Has ever heard the name "Old Blue,"
Whose fame through all this region rung
In those old days when I was young!

"Bring forth the horse!" Alas! he showed
Not like the one Mazeppa rode;
Scant-maned, sharp-backed, and shaky-kneed,
The wreck of what was once a steed,
Lips thin, eyes hollow, stiff in joints;

Yet not without his knowing points.
The sexton laughing in his sleeve,
As if 't were all a make-believe,
Led forth the horse, and as he laughed
Unhitched the breeching from a shaft,
Unclasped the rusty belt beneath,
Drew forth the snaffle from his teeth,
Slipped off his head-stall, set him free
From strap and rein,—a sight to see!

So worn, so lean in every limb,
It can't be they are saddling him!
It is! his back the pig-skin strides
And flaps his lank, rheumatic sides;
With look of mingled scorn and mirth
They buckle round the saddle-girth;
With horsey wink and saucy toss
A youngster throws his leg across,
And so, his rider on his back,
They lead him, limping, to the track,
Far up behind the starting-point,
To limber out each stiffened joint.

As through the jeering crowd he past,
One pitying look Old Hiram cast;
"Go it, ye cripple, while ye can!"
Cried out unsentimental Dan;
"A Fast-Day dinner for the crows!"
Budd Doble's scoffing shout arose.

Slowly, as when the walking-beam
First feels the gathering head of steam,
With warning cough and threatening wheeze
The stiff old charger crooks his knees;
At first with cautious step sedate,
As if he dragged a coach of state
He's not a colt; he knows full well
That time is weight and sure to tell;
No horse so sturdy but he fears
The handicap of twenty years.

As through the throng on either hand
The old horse nears the judges' stand,
Beneath his jockey's feather-weight

He warms a little to his gait,
And now and then a step is tried
That hints of something like a stride.

    "Go!" —Through his ear the summons stung
As if a battle-trump had rung;
The slumbering instincts long unstirred
Start at the old familiar word;
It thrills like flame through every limb, —
What mean his twenty years to him?
The savage blow his rider dealt
Fell on his hollow flanks unfelt;
The spur that pricked his staring hide
Unheeded tore his bleeding side;
Alike to him are spur and rein, —
He steps a five-year-old again!

    Before the quarter pole was past,
Old Hiram said, "He's going fast."
Long ere the quarter was a half,
The chuckling crowd had ceased to laugh;
Tighter his frightened jockey clung
As in a mighty stride he swung,
The gravel flying in his track,
His neck stretched out, his ears laid back,
His tail extended all the while
Behind him like a rat-tail file!
Off went a shoe, —away it spun,
Shot like a bullet from a gun;

    The quaking jockey shapes a prayer
From scraps of oaths he used to swear;
He drops his whip, he drops his rein,
He clutches fiercely for a mane;
He'll lose his hold—he sways and reels—
He'll slide beneath those trampling heels!
The knees of many a horseman quake,
The flowers on many a bonnet shake,
And shouts arise from left and right,
"Stick on! Stick on!" "Hould tight! Hould tight!"
"Cling round his neck and don't let go—"
"That pace can't hold—there! steady! whoa!"
But like the sable steed that bore
The spectral lover of Lenore,

His nostrils snorting foam and fire,
No stretch his bony limbs can tire;
And now the stand he rushes by,
And "Stop him!—stop him!" is the cry.
Stand back! he 's only just begun—
He's having out three heats in one!

     "Don't rush in front! he'll smash your brains;
But follow up and grab the reins!"
Old Hiram spoke. Dan Pfeiffer heard,
And sprang impatient at the word;
Budd Doble started on his bay,
Old Hiram followed on his gray,
And off they spring, and round they go,
The fast ones doing "all they know."
Look! twice they follow at his heels,
As round the circling course he wheels,
And whirls with him that clinging boy
Like Hector round the walls of Troy;
Still on, and on, the third time round
They're tailing off! they're losing ground!
Budd Doble's nag begins to fail!
Dan Pfeiffer's sorrel whisks his tail!
And see! in spite of whip and shout,
Old Hiram's mare is giving out!
Now for the finish! at the turn,
The old horse—all the rest astern—
Comes swinging in, with easy trot;
By Jove! he's distanced all the lot!

     That trot no mortal could explain;
Some said, "Old Dutchman come again!"
Some took his time,—at least they tried,
But what it was could none decide;
One said he couldn't understand
What happened to his second hand;
One said 2.10; that could n't be—
More like two twenty-two or three;
Old Hiram settled it at last;
"The time was two—too dee-vel-ish fast!"

The parson's horse had won the bet;
It cost him something of a sweat;
Back in the one-horse shay he went;
The parson wondered what it meant,
And murmured, with a mild surprise
And pleasant twinkle of the eyes,
That funeral must have been a trick,
Or corpses drive at double-quick;
I should n't wonder, I declare,
If brother—Jehu—made the prayer!

And this is all I have to say
About that tough old trotting bay,
Huddup! Huddup! G'lang! Good day!
Moral for which this tale is told
A horse can trot, for all he 's old.

AN APPEAL FOR "THE OLD SOUTH"

"While stands the Coliseum, Rome shall stand;
When falls the Coliseum, Rome shall fall."

FULL sevenscore years our city's pride—
The comely Southern spire—
Has cast its shadow, and defied
The storm, the foe, the fire;
Sad is the sight our eyes behold;
Woe to the three-hilled town,
When through the land the tale is told—
"The brave 'Old South' is down!"

Let darkness blot the starless dawn
That hears our children tell,
"Here rose the walls, now wrecked and gone,
Our fathers loved so well;
Here, while his brethren stood aloof,
The herald's blast was blown
That shook St. Stephen's pillared roof
And rocked King George's throne!

"The home-bound wanderer of the main
Looked from his deck afar,
To where the gilded, glittering vane
Shone like the evening star,
And pilgrim feet from every clime
The floor with reverence trod,
Where holy memories made sublime
The shrine of Freedom's God!"

The darkened skies, alas! have seen
Our monarch tree laid low,
And spread in ruins o'er the green,

But Nature struck the blow;
No scheming thrift its downfall planned,
It felt no edge of steel,
No soulless hireling raised his hand
The deadly stroke to deal.

    In bridal garlands, pale and mute,
Still pleads the storied tower;
These are the blossoms, but the fruit
Awaits the golden shower;
The spire still greets the morning sun, —
Say, shall it stand or fall?
Help, ere the spoiler has begun!
Help, each, and God help all!

THE FIRST FAN

**READ AT A MEETING OF THE BOSTON
BRIC-A-BRAC CLUB, FEBRUARY 21, 1877**

WHEN rose the cry "Great Pan is dead!"
And Jove's high palace closed its portal,
The fallen gods, before they fled,
Sold out their frippery to a mortal.

"To whom?" you ask. I ask of you.
The answer hardly needs suggestion;
Of course it was the Wandering Jew, —
How could you put me such a question?

A purple robe, a little worn,
The Thunderer deigned himself to offer;
The bearded wanderer laughed in scorn, —
You know he always was a scoffer.

"Vife shillins! 't is a monstrous price;
Say two and six and further talk shun."
"Take it," cried Jove; "we can't be nice, —
'T would fetch twice that at Leonard's auction."

The ice was broken; up they came,
All sharp for bargains, god and goddess,
Each ready with the price to name
For robe or head-dress, scarf or bodice.

First Juno, out of temper, too, —
Her queenly forehead somewhat cloudy;
Then Pallas in her stockings blue,
Imposing, but a little dowdy.

The scowling queen of heaven unrolled
Before the Jew a threadbare turban
"Three shillings." "One. 'T will suit some old
Terrific feminine suburban."

But as for Pallas,—how to tell
In seemly phrase a fact so shocking?
She pointed,—pray excuse me,—well,
She pointed to her azure stocking.

And if the honest truth were told,
Its heel confessed the need of darning;
"Gods!" low-bred Vulcan cried, "behold!
There! that's what comes of too much larning!"

Pale Proserpine came groping round,
Her pupils dreadfully dilated
With too much living underground,—
A residence quite overrated;

This kerchief's what you want, I know,—
Don't cheat poor Venus of her cestus,—
You'll find it handy when you go
To—you know where; it's pure asbestus.

Then Phoebus of the silverr bow,
And Hebe, dimpled as a baby,
And Dian with the breast of snow,
Chaser and chased—and caught, it may be:

One took the quiver from her back,
One held the cap he spent the night in,
And one a bit of bric-a-brac,
Such as the gods themselves delight in.

Then Mars, the foe of human kind,
Strode up and showed his suit of armor;
So none at last was left behind
Save Venus, the celestial charmer.

Poor Venus! What had she to sell?
For all she looked so fresh and jaunty,
Her wardrobe, as I blush' to tell,
Already seemed but quite too scanty.

Her gems were sold, her sandals gone,—
She always would be rash and flighty,—
Her winter garments all in pawn,
Alas for charming Aphrodite.

The lady of a thousand loves,
The darling of the old religion,

Had only left of all the doves
That drew her car one fan-tailed pigeon.

How oft upon her finger-tips
He perched, afraid of Cupid's arrow,
Or kissed her on the rosebud lips,
Like Roman Lesbia's loving sparrow!

"My bird, I want your train," she cried;
"Come, don't let's have a fuss about it;
I'll make it beauty's pet and pride,
And you'll be better off without it.

"So vulgar! Have you noticed, pray,
An earthly belle or dashing bride walk,
And how her flounces track her way,
Like slimy serpents on the sidewalk?

"A lover's heart it quickly cools;
In mine it kindles up enough rage
To wring their necks. How can such fools
Ask men to vote for woman suffrage?"

The goddess spoke, and gently stripped
Her bird of every caudal feather;
A strand of gold-bright hair she clipped,
And bound the glossy plumes together,

And lo, the Fan! for beauty's hand,
The lovely queen of beauty made it;
The price she named was hard to stand,
But Venus smiled: the Hebrew paid it.

Jove, Juno, Venus, where are you?
Mars, Mercury, Phoebus, Neptune, Saturn?
But o'er the world the Wandering Jew
Has borne the Fan's celestial pattern.

So everywhere we find the Fan, —
In lonely isles of the Pacific,
In farthest China and Japan, —
Wherever suns are sudorific.

Nay, even the oily Esquimaux
In summer court its cooling breezes, —
In fact, in every clime 't is so,
No matter if it fries or freezes.

And since from Aphrodite's dove
The pattern of the fan was given,
No wonder that it breathes of love
And wafts the perfumed gales of heaven!

Before this new Pandora's gift
In slavery woman's tyrant kept her,
But now he kneels her glove to lift, —
The fan is mightier than the sceptre.

The tap it gives how arch and sly!
The breath it wakes how fresh and grateful!
Behind its shield how soft the sigh!
The whispered tale of shame how fateful!

Its empire shadows every throne
And every shore that man is tost on;
It rules the lords of every zone,
Nay, even the bluest blood of Boston!

But every one that swings to-night,
Of fairest shape, from farthest region,
May trace its pedigree aright
To Aphrodite's fan-tailed pigeon.

TO R. B. H.

AT THE DINNER TO THE PRESIDENT, BOSTON, JUNE 26, 1877

How to address him? awkward, it is true
Call him "Great Father," as the Red Men do?
Borrow some title? this is not the place
That christens men Your Highness and Your Grace;
We tried such names as these awhile, you know,
But left them off a century ago.

His Majesty? We've had enough of that
Besides, that needs a crown; he wears a hat.
What if, to make the nicer ears content,
We say His Honesty, the President?

Sir, we believed you honest, truthful, brave,
When to your hands their precious trust we gave,
And we have found you better than we knew,
Braver, and not less honest, not less true!
So every heart has opened, every hand
Tingles with welcome, and through all the land
All voices greet you in one broad acclaim,
Healer of strife! Has earth a nobler name?

What phrases mean you do not need to learn;
We must be civil, and they serve our turn
"Your most obedient humble" means—means what?
Something the well-bred signer just is not.

Yet there are tokens, sir, you must believe;
There is one language never can deceive
The lover knew it when the maiden smiled;

The mother knows it when she clasps her child;
Voices may falter, trembling lips turn pale,
Words grope and stumble; this will tell their tale
Shorn of all rhetoric, bare of all pretence,
But radiant, warm, with Nature's eloquence.
Look in our eyes! Your welcome waits you there,—
North, South, East, West, from all and everywhere!

THE SHIP OF STATE

A SENTIMENT

This "sentiment" was read on the same occasion as the
"Family Record," which immediately follows it. The latter
poem is the dutiful tribute of a son to his father and his father's
ancestors, residents of Woodstock from its first settlement.

THE Ship of State! above her skies are blue,
But still she rocks a little, it is true,
And there are passengers whose faces white
Show they don't feel as happy as they might;
Yet on the whole her crew are quite content,
Since its wild fury the typhoon has spent,
And willing, if her pilot thinks it best,
To head a little nearer south by west.
And this they feel: the ship came too near wreck,
In the long quarrel for the quarter-deck,
Now when she glides serenely on her way, —
The shallows past where dread explosives lay, —
The stiff obstructive's churlish game to try
Let sleeping dogs and still torpedoes lie!
And so I give you all the Ship of State;
Freedom's last venture is her priceless freight;
God speed her, keep her, bless her, while she steers
Amid the breakers of unsounded years;
Lead her through danger's paths with even keel,
And guide the honest hand that holds her wheel!

WOODSTOCK, CONN., July 4, 1877.

A FAMILY RECORD

WOODSTOCK, CONN., JULY 4, 1877

NOT to myself this breath of vesper song,
Not to these patient friends, this kindly throng,
Not to this hallowed morning, though it be
Our summer Christmas, Freedom's jubilee,
When every summit, topmast, steeple, tower,
That owns her empire spreads her starry flower,
Its blood-streaked leaves in heaven's benignant dew
Washed clean from every crimson stain they knew, —
No, not to these the passing thrills belong
That steal my breath to hush themselves with song.
These moments all are memory's; I have come
To speak with lips that rather should be dumb;
For what are words? At every step I tread
The dust that wore the footprints of the dead
But for whose life my life had never known
This faded vesture which it calls its own.
Here sleeps my father's sire, and they who gave
That earlier life here found their peaceful grave.
In days gone by I sought the hallowed ground;
Climbed yon long slope; the sacred spot I found
Where all unsullied lies the winter snow,
Where all ungathered spring's pale violets blow,
And tracked from stone to stone the Saxon name
That marks the blood I need not blush to claim,
Blood such as warmed the Pilgrim sons of toil,
Who held from God the charter of the soil.
I come an alien to your hills and plains,
Yet feel your birthright tingling in my veins;
Mine are this changing prospect's sun and shade,
In full-blown summer's bridal pomp arrayed;
Mine these fair hillsides and the vales between;
Mine the sweet streams that lend their brightening green;
I breathed your air — the sunlit landscape smiled;

I touch your soil—it knows its children's child;
Throned in my heart your heritage is mine;
I claim it all by memory's right divine
Waking, I dream. Before my vacant eyes
In long procession shadowy forms arise;
Far through the vista of the silent years
I see a venturous band; the pioneers,
Who let the sunlight through the forest's gloom,
Who bade the harvest wave, the garden bloom.
Hark! loud resounds the bare-armed settler's axe,
See where the stealthy panther left his tracks!
As fierce, as stealthy creeps the skulking foe
With stone-tipped shaft and sinew-corded bow;
Soon shall he vanish from his ancient reign,
Leave his last cornfield to the coming train,
Quit the green margin of the wave he drinks,
For haunts that hide the wild-cat and the lynx.

But who the Youth his glistening axe that swings
To smite the pine that shows a hundred rings?
His features?—something in his look I find
That calls the semblance of my race to mind.
His name?—my own; and that which goes before
The same that once the loved disciple bore.
Young, brave, discreet, the father of a line
Whose voiceless lives have found a voice in mine;
Thinned by unnumbered currents though they be,
Thanks for the ruddy drops I claim from thee!

The seasons pass; the roses come and go;
Snows fall and melt; the waters freeze and flow;
The boys are men; the girls, grown tall and fair,
Have found their mates; a gravestone here and there
Tells where the fathers lie; the silvered hair
Of some bent patriarch yet recalls the time
That saw his feet the northern hillside climb,
A pilgrim from the pilgrims far away,
The godly men, the dwellers by the bay.
On many a hearthstone burns the cheerful fire;
The schoolhouse porch, the heavenward pointing spire
Proclaim in letters every eye can read,

Knowledge and Faith, the new world's simple creed.
Hush! 't is the Sabbath's silence-stricken morn
No feet must wander through the tasselled corn;
No merry children laugh around the door,
No idle playthings strew the sanded floor;
The law of Moses lays its awful ban
On all that stirs; here comes the tithing-man
At last the solemn hour of worship calls;
Slowly they gather in the sacred walls;
Man in his strength and age with knotted staff,
And boyhood aching for its week-day laugh,
The toil-worn mother with the child she leads,
The maiden, lovely in her golden beads, —
The popish symbols round her neck she wears,
But on them counts her lovers, not her prayers, —
Those youths in homespun suits and ribboned queues,
Whose hearts are beating in the high-backed pews.
The pastor rises; looks along the seats
With searching eye; each wonted face he meets;
Asks heavenly guidance; finds the chapter's place
That tells some tale of Israel's stubborn race;
Gives out the sacred song; all voices join,
For no quartette extorts their scanty coin;
Then while both hands their black-gloved palms display,
Lifts his gray head, and murmurs, "Let us pray!"
And pray he does! as one that never fears
To plead unanswered by the God that hears;
What if he dwells on many a fact as though
Some things Heaven knew not which it ought to know, —
Thanks God for all his favors past, and yet,
Tells Him there's something He must not forget;
Such are the prayers his people love to hear, —
See how the Deacon slants his listening ear!
What! look once more! Nay, surely there I trace
The hinted outlines of a well-known face!
Not those the lips for laughter to beguile,
Yet round their corners lurks an embryo smile,
The same on other lips my childhood knew
That scarce the Sabbath's mastery could subdue.

Him too my lineage gives me leave to claim, —
The good, grave man that bears the Psalmist's name.

And still in ceaseless round the seasons passed;
Spring piped her carol; Autumn blew his blast;
Babes waxed to manhood; manhood shrunk to age;
Life's worn-out players tottered off the stage;
The few are many; boys have grown to men
Since Putnam dragged the wolf from Pomfret's den;
Our new-old Woodstock is a thriving town;
Brave are her children; faithful to the crown;
Her soldiers' steel the savage redskin knows;
Their blood has crimsoned his Canadian snows.
And now once more along the quiet vale
Rings the dread call that turns the mothers pale;
Full well they know the valorous heat that runs
In every pulse-beat of their loyal sons;
Who would not bleed in good King George's cause
When England's lion shows his teeth and claws?
With glittering firelocks on the village green
In proud array a martial band is seen;
You know what names those ancient rosters hold, —
Whose belts were buckled when the drum-beat rolled, —
But mark their Captain! tell us, who is he?
On his brown face that same old look I see
Yes! from the homestead's still retreat he came,
Whose peaceful owner bore the Psalmist's name;
The same his own. Well, Israel's glorious king
Who struck the harp could also whirl the sling, —
Breathe in his song a penitential sigh
And smite the sons of Amalek hip and thigh:
These shared their task; one deaconed out the psalm,
One slashed the scalping hell-hounds of calm;
The praying father's pious work is done,
Now sword in hand steps forth the fighting son.
On many a field he fought in wilds afar;
See on his swarthy cheek the bullet's scar!
There hangs a murderous tomahawk; beneath,
Without its blade, a knife's embroidered sheath;
Save for the stroke his trusty weapon dealt
His scalp had dangled at their owner's belt;

But not for him such fate; he lived to see
The bloodier strife that made our nation free,
To serve with willing toil, with skilful hand,
The war-worn saviors of the bleeding land.
His wasting life to others' needs he gave, —
Sought rest in home and found it in the grave.
See where the stones life's brief memorials keep,
The tablet telling where he "fell on sleep," —
Watched by a winged cherub's rayless eye, —
A scroll above that says we all must die, —
Those saddening lines beneath, the "Night-Thoughts" lent:
So stands the Soldier's, Surgeon's monument.
Ah! at a glance my filial eye divines
The scholar son in those remembered lines.

      The Scholar Son. His hand my footsteps led.
No more the dim unreal past I tread.
O thou whose breathing form was once so dear,
Whose cheering voice was music to my ear,
Art thou not with me as my feet pursue
The village paths so well thy boyhood knew,
Along the tangled margin of the stream
Whose murmurs blended with thine infant dream,
Or climb the hill, or thread the wooded vale,
Or seek the wave where gleams yon distant sail,
Or the old homestead's narrowed bounds explore,
Where sloped the roof that sheds the rains no more,
Where one last relic still remains to tell
Here stood thy home, — the memory-haunted well,
Whose waters quench a deeper thirst than thine,
Changed at my lips to sacramental wine, —
Art thou not with me, as I fondly trace
The scanty records of thine honored race,
Call up the forms that earlier years have known,
And spell the legend of each slanted stone?
With thoughts of thee my loving verse began,
Not for the critic's curious eye to scan,
Not for the many listeners, but the few
Whose fathers trod the paths my fathers knew;
Still in my heart thy loved remembrance burns;

Still to my lips thy cherished name returns;
Could I but feel thy gracious presence near
Amid the groves that once to thee were dear
Could but my trembling lips with mortal speech
Thy listening ear for one brief moment reach!
How vain the dream! The pallid voyager's track
No sign betrays; he sends no message back.
No word from thee since evening's shadow fell
On thy cold forehead with my long farewell,—
Now from the margin of the silent sea,
Take my last offering ere I cross to thee!

THE IRON GATE

AND OTHER POEMS

1877-1881

THE IRON GATE

Read at the Breakfast given in honor of Dr.
Holmes's Seventieth Birthday by the publishers of the
"Atlantic Monthly," Boston, December 3, 1879.

WHERE is this patriarch you are kindly greeting?
Not unfamiliar to my ear his name,
Nor yet unknown to many a joyous meeting
In days long vanished,—is he still the same,

Or changed by years, forgotten and forgetting,
Dull-eared, dim-sighted, slow of speech and thought,
Still o'er the sad, degenerate present fretting,
Where all goes wrong, and nothing as it ought?

Old age, the graybeard! Well, indeed, I know him,—
Shrunk, tottering, bent, of aches and ills the prey;
In sermon, story, fable, picture, poem,
Oft have I met him from my earliest day.

In my old AEsop, toiling with his bundle,—
His load of sticks,—politely asking Death,
Who comes when called for,—would he lug or trundle
His fagot for him?—he was scant of breath.

And sad "Ecclesiastes, or the Preacher,"—
Has he not stamped the image on my soul,
In that last chapter, where the worn-out Teacher
Sighs o'er the loosened cord, the broken bowl?

Yes, long, indeed, I've known him at a distance,
And now my lifted door-latch shows him here;
I take his shrivelled hand without resistance,
And find him smiling as his step draws near.

What though of gilded baubles he bereaves us,
Dear to the heart of youth, to manhood's prime;
Think of the calm he brings, the wealth he leaves us,
The hoarded spoils, the legacies of time!

Altars once flaming, still with incense fragrant,
Passion's uneasy nurslings rocked asleep,
Hope's anchor faster, wild desire less vagrant,
Life's flow less noisy, but the stream how deep!

Still as the silver cord gets worn and slender,
Its lightened task-work tugs with lessening strain,
Hands get more helpful, voices, grown more tender,
Soothe with their softened tones the slumberous brain.

Youth longs and manhood strives, but age remembers,
Sits by the raked-up ashes of the past,
Spreads its thin hands above the whitening embers
That warm its creeping life-blood till the last.

Dear to its heart is every loving token
That comes unbidden ere its pulse grows cold,
Ere the last lingering ties of life are broken,
Its labors ended and its story told.

Ah, while around us rosy youth rejoices,
For us the sorrow-laden breezes sigh,
And through the chorus of its jocund voices
Throbs the sharp note of misery's hopeless cry.

As on the gauzy wings of fancy flying
From some far orb I track our watery sphere,
Home of the struggling, suffering, doubting, dying,
The silvered globule seems a glistening tear.

But Nature lends her mirror of illusion
To win from saddening scenes our age-dimmed eyes,
And misty day-dreams blend in sweet confusion
The wintry landscape and the summer skies.

So when the iron portal shuts behind us,
And life forgets us in its noise and whirl,
Visions that shunned the glaring noonday find us,
And glimmering starlight shows the gates of pearl.

I come not here your morning hour to sadden,
A limping pilgrim, leaning on his staff, —

I, who have never deemed it sin to gladden
This vale of sorrows with a wholesome laugh.

If word of mine another's gloom has brightened,
Through my dumb lips the heaven-sent message came;
If hand of mine another's task has lightened,
It felt the guidance that it dares not claim.

But, O my gentle sisters, O my brothers,
These thick-sown snow-flakes hint of toil's release;
These feebler pulses bid me leave to others
The tasks once welcome; evening asks for peace.

Time claims his tribute; silence now is golden;
Let me not vex the too long suffering lyre;
Though to your love untiring still beholden,
The curfew tells me—cover up the fire.

And now with grateful smile and accents cheerful,
And warmer heart than look or word can tell,
In simplest phrase—these traitorous eyes are tearful—
Thanks, Brothers, Sisters,—Children,—and farewell!

VESTIGIA QUINQUE RETRORSUM

AN ACADEMIC POEM

1829-1879

Read at the Commencement Dinner of the Alumni of Harvard
University, June 25, 1879.

WHILE fond, sad memories all around us throng,
Silence were sweeter than the sweetest song;
Yet when the leaves are green and heaven is blue,
The choral tribute of the grove is due,
And when the lengthening nights have chilled the skies,
We fain would hear the song-bird ere be flies,
And greet with kindly welcome, even as now,
The lonely minstrel on his leafless bough.

This is our golden year,—its golden day;
Its bridal memories soon must pass away;
Soon shall its dying music cease to ring,
And every year must loose some silver string,
Till the last trembling chords no longer thrill,—
Hands all at rest and hearts forever still.

A few gray heads have joined the forming line;
We hear our summons,—"Class of 'Twenty-Nine!"
Close on the foremost, and, alas, how few!
Are these "The Boys" our dear old Mother knew?
Sixty brave swimmers. Twenty—something more—
Have passed the stream and reached this frosty shore!

How near the banks these fifty years divide
When memory crosses with a single stride!
'T is the first year of stern "Old Hickory" 's rule
When our good Mother lets us out of school,
Half glad, half sorrowing, it must be confessed,
To leave her quiet lap, her bounteous breast,
Armed with our dainty, ribbon-tied degrees,
Pleased and yet pensive, exiles and A. B.'s.

Look back, O comrades, with your faded eyes,
And see the phantoms as I bid them rise.
Whose smile is that? Its pattern Nature gave,
A sunbeam dancing in a dimpled wave;
KIRKLAND alone such grace from Heaven could win,
His features radiant as the soul within;
That smile would let him through Saint Peter's gate
While sad-eyed martyrs had to stand and wait.
Here flits mercurial *Farrar* ; standing there,
See mild, benignant, cautious, learned *Ware* ,
And sturdy, patient, faithful, honest *Hedge* ,
Whose grinding logic gave our wits their edge;
Ticknor , with honeyed voice and courtly grace;
And *Willard* , larynxed like a double bass;
And *Channing* , with his bland, superior look,
Cool as a moonbeam on a frozen brook,

While the pale student, shivering in his shoes,
Sees from his theme the turgid rhetoric ooze;
And the born soldier, fate decreed to wreak
His martial manhood on a class in Greek,
Popkin ! How that explosive name recalls
The grand old Busby of our ancient halls
Such faces looked from Skippon's grim platoons,
Such figures rode with Ireton's stout dragoons:
He gave his strength to learning's gentle charms,
But every accent sounded "Shoulder arms!"

Names,—empty names! Save only here and there
Some white-haired listener, dozing in his chair,
Starts at the sound he often used to hear,
And upward slants his Sunday-sermon ear.
And we—our blooming manhood we regain;
Smiling we join the long Commencement train,
One point first battled in discussion hot,—
Shall we wear gowns? and settled: We will not.
How strange the scene,—that noisy boy-debate
Where embryo-speakers learn to rule the State!
This broad-browed youth, sedate and sober-eyed,
Shall wear the ermined robe at Taney's side;
And he, the stripling, smooth of face and slight,
Whose slender form scarce intercepts the light,
Shall rule the Bench where Parsons gave the law,

And sphinx-like sat uncouth, majestic Shaw
Ah, many a star has shed its fatal ray
On names we loved—our brothers—where are they?

Nor these alone; our hearts in silence claim
Names not less dear, unsyllabled by fame.

How brief the space! and yet it sweeps us back
Far, far along our new-born history's track
Five strides like this;—the sachem rules the land;
The Indian wigwams cluster where we stand.

The second. Lo! a scene of deadly strife—
A nation struggling into infant life;
Not yet the fatal game at Yorktown won
Where failing Empire fired its sunset gun.
LANGDON sits restless in the ancient chair,—
Harvard's grave Head,—these echoes heard his prayer
When from yon mansion, dear to memory still,
The banded yeomen marched for Bunker's Hill.
Count on the grave triennial's thick-starred roll
What names were numbered on the lengthening scroll,—
Not unfamiliar in our ears they ring,—
Winthrop, Hale, Eliot, Everett, Dexter, Tyng.

Another stride. Once more at 'twenty-nine,—
GOD SAVE KING GEORGE, the Second of his line!
And is Sir Isaac living? Nay, not so,—
He followed Flainsteed two short years ago,—
And what about the little hump-backed man
Who pleased the bygone days of good Queen Anne?
What, Pope? another book he's just put out,—
"The Dunciad,"—witty, but profane, no doubt.

Where's Cotton Mather? he was always here.
And so he would be, but he died last year.
Who is this preacher our Northampton claims,
Whose rhetoric blazes with sulphureous flames
And torches stolen from Tartarean mines?
Edwards, the salamander of divines.
A deep, strong nature, pure and undefiled;
Faith, firm as his who stabbed his sleeping child;
Alas for him who blindly strays apart,
And seeking God has lost his human heart!
Fall where they might, no flying cinders caught

These sober halls where WADSWORTH ruled and
taught.

One footstep more; the fourth receding stride
Leaves the round century on the nearer side.
GOD SAVE KING CHARLES! God knows that pleasant knave
His grace will find it hard enough to save.
Ten years and more, and now the Plague, the Fire,
Talk of all tongues, at last begin to tire;
One fear prevails, all other frights forgot, —
White lips are whispering, — hark! The Popish Plot!
Happy New England, from such troubles free
In health and peace beyond the stormy sea!
No Romish daggers threat her children's throats,
No gibbering nightmare mutters "Titus Oates;"
Philip is slain, the Quaker graves are green,
Not yet the witch has entered on the scene;
Happy our Harvard; pleased her graduates four;
URIAN OAKES the name their parchments bore.

Two centuries past, our hurried feet arrive
At the last footprint of the scanty five;
Take the fifth stride; our wandering eyes explore
A tangled forest on a trackless shore;
Here, where we stand, the savage sorcerer howls,
The wild cat snarls, the stealthy gray wolf prowls,
The slouching bear, perchance the trampling moose
Starts the brown squaw and scares her red pappoose;
At every step the lurking foe is near;
His Demons reign; God has no temple here!

Lift up your eyes! behold these pictured walls;
Look where the flood of western glory falls
Through the great sunflower disk of blazing panes
In ruby, saffron, azure, emerald stains;
With reverent step the marble pavement tread
Where our proud Mother's martyr-roll is read;
See the great halls that cluster, gathering round
This lofty shrine with holiest memories crowned;
See the fair Matron in her summer bower,
Fresh as a rose in bright perennial flower;
Read on her standard, always in the van,
"TRUTH," — the one word that makes a slave a man;

Think whose the hands that fed her altar-fires,
Then count the debt we owe our scholar-sires!

  Brothers, farewell! the fast declining ray
Fades to the twilight of our golden day;
Some lesson yet our wearied brains may learn,
Some leaves, perhaps, in life's thin volume turn.
How few they seem as in our waning age
We count them backwards to the title-page!
Oh let us trust with holy men of old
Not all the story here begun is told;
So the tired spirit, waiting to be freed,
On life's last leaf with tranquil eye shall read
By the pale glimmer of the torch reversed,
Not Finis, but *The End of Volume First* !

MY AVIARY

Through my north window, in the wintry weather,—
My airy oriel on the river shore,—
I watch the sea-fowl as they flock together
Where late the boatman flashed his dripping oar.

The gull, high floating, like a sloop unladen,
Lets the loose water waft him as it will;
The duck, round-breasted as a rustic maiden,
Paddles and plunges, busy, busy still.

I see the solemn gulls in council sitting
On some broad ice-floe pondering long and late,
While overhead the home-bound ducks are flitting,
And leave the tardy conclave in debate,

Those weighty questions in their breasts revolving
Whose deeper meaning science never learns,
Till at some reverend elder's look dissolving,
The speechless senate silently adjourns.

But when along the waves the shrill north-easter
Shrieks through the laboring coaster's shrouds "Beware!"
The pale bird, kindling like a Christmas feaster
When some wild chorus shakes the vinous air,

Flaps from the leaden wave in fierce rejoicing,
Feels heaven's dumb lightning thrill his torpid nerves,
Now on the blast his whistling plumage poising,
Now wheeling, whirling in fantastic curves.

Such is our gull; a gentleman of leisure,
Less fleshed than feathered; bagged you'll find him such;
His virtue silence; his employment pleasure;
Not bad to look at, and not good for much.

What of our duck? He has some high-bred cousins,—
His Grace the Canvas-back, My Lord the Brant,—
Anas and Anser,—both served up by dozens,
At Boston's Rocher, half-way to Nahant.

As for himself, he seems alert and thriving,—
Grubs up a living somehow—what, who knows?
Crabs? mussels? weeds?—Look quick! there 's one just diving!
Flop! Splash! his white breast glistens—down he goes!

And while he 's under—just about a minute—
I take advantage of the fact to say
His fishy carcase has no virtue in it
The gunning idiot's worthless hire to pay.

Shrewd is our bird; not easy to outwit him!
Sharp is the outlook of those pin-head eyes;
Still, he is mortal and a shot may hit him,
One cannot always miss him if he tries.

He knows you! "sportsmen" from suburban alleys,
Stretched under seaweed in the treacherous punt;
Knows every lazy, shiftless lout that sallies
Forth to waste powder—as he says, to "hunt."

I watch you with a patient satisfaction,
Well pleased to discount your predestined luck;
The float that figures in your sly transaction
Will carry back a goose, but not a duck.

Look! there's a young one, dreaming not of danger;
Sees a flat log come floating down the stream;
Stares undismayed upon the harmless stranger;
Ah! were all strangers harmless as they seem!

Habet ! a leaden shower his breast has shattered;
Vainly he flutters, not again to rise;
His soft white plumes along the waves are scattered;
Helpless the wing that braved the tempest lies.

He sees his comrades high above him flying
To seek their nests among the island reeds;
Strong is their flight; all lonely he is lying
Washed by the crimsoned water as he bleeds.

O Thou who carest for the falling sparrow,
Canst Thou the sinless sufferer's pang forget?
Or is thy dread account-book's page so narrow
Its one long column scores thy creatures' debt?

Poor gentle guest, by nature kindly cherished,
A world grows dark with thee in blinding death;

One little gasp—thy universe has perished,
Wrecked by the idle thief who stole thy breath!

Is this the whole sad story of creation,
Lived by its breathing myriads o'er and o'er,—
One glimpse of day, then black annihilation,—
A sunlit passage to a sunless shore?

Give back our faith, ye mystery-solving lynxes!
Robe us once more in heaven-aspiring creeds
Happier was dreaming Egypt with her sphinxes,
The stony convent with its cross and beads!

How often gazing where a bird reposes,
Rocked on the wavelets, drifting with the tide,
I lose myself in strange metempsychosis
And float a sea-fowl at a sea-fowl's side;

From rain, hail, snow in feathery mantle muffled,
Clear-eyed, strong-limbed, with keenest sense to hear
My mate soft murmuring, who, with plumes unruffled,
Where'er I wander still is nestling near;

The great blue hollow like a garment o'er me;
Space all unmeasured, unrecorded time;
While seen with inward eye moves on before me
Thought's pictured train in wordless pantomime.

A voice recalls me.—From my window turning
I find myself a plumeless biped still;
No beak, no claws, no sign of wings discerning,—
In fact with nothing bird-like but my quill.

ON THE THRESHOLD

INTRODUCTION TO A COLLECTION OF POEMS BYDIFFERENT AUTHORS

AN usher standing at the door
I show my white rosette;
A smile of welcome, nothing more,
Will pay my trifling debt;
Why should I bid you idly wait
Like lovers at the swinging gate?

Can I forget the wedding guest?
The veteran of the sea?
In vain the listener smites his breast, —
"There was a ship," cries he!
Poor fasting victim, stunned and pale,
He needs must listen to the tale.

He sees the gilded throng within,
The sparkling goblets gleam,
The music and the merry din
Through every window stream,
But there he shivers in the cold
Till all the crazy dream is told.

Not mine the graybeard's glittering eye
That held his captive still
To hold my silent prisoners by
And let me have my will;
Nay, I were like the three-years' child,
To think you could be so beguiled!

My verse is but the curtain's fold
That hides the painted scene,
The mist by morning's ray unrolled

That veils the meadow's green,
The cloud that needs must drift away
To show the rose of opening day.

    See, from the tinkling rill you hear
In hollowed palm I bring
These scanty drops, but ah, how near
The founts that heavenward spring!
Thus, open wide the gates are thrown
And founts and flowers are all your own!

TO GEORGE PEABODY

DANVERS, 1866

BANKRUPT! our pockets inside out!
Empty of words to speak his praises!
Worcester and Webster up the spout!
Dead broke of laudatory phrases!
Yet why with flowery speeches tease,
With vain superlatives distress him?
Has language better words than these?
THE FRIEND OF ALL HIS RACE, GOD BLESS HIM!

A simple prayer—but words more sweet
By human lips were never uttered,
Since Adam left the country seat
Where angel wings around him fluttered.
The old look on with tear-dimmed eyes,
The children cluster to caress him,
And every voice unbidden cries,
THE FRIEND OF ALL HIS RACE, GOD BLESS HIM!

AT THE PAPYRUS CLUB

A LOVELY show for eyes to see
I looked upon this morning,—
A bright-hued, feathered company
Of nature's own adorning;
But ah! those minstrels would not sing
A listening ear while I lent,—
The lark sat still and preened his wing,
The nightingale was silent;
I longed for what they gave me not—
Their warblings sweet and fluty,
But grateful still for all I got
I thanked them for their beauty.

A fairer vision meets my view
Of Claras, Margarets, Marys,
In silken robes of varied hue,
Like bluebirds and canaries;
The roses blush, the jewels gleam,
The silks and satins glisten,
The black eyes flash, the blue eyes beam,
We look—and then we listen
Behold the flock we cage to-night—
Was ever such a capture?
To see them is a pure delight;
To hear them—ah! what rapture!

Methinks I hear Delilah's laugh
At Samson bound in fetters;
"We captured!" shrieks each lovelier half,
"Men think themselves our betters!
We push the bolt, we turn the key
On warriors, poets, sages,

Too happy, all of them, to be
Locked in our golden cages!"
Beware! the boy with bandaged eyes
Has flung away his blinder;

He 's lost his mother—so he cries—
And here he knows he'll find her:
The rogue! 't is but a new device,—
Look out for flying arrows
Whene'er the birds of Paradise
Are perched amid the sparrows!

FOR WHITTIER'S SEVENTIETH BIRTHDAY

DECEMBER 17, 1877

I BELIEVE that the copies of verses I've spun,
Like Scheherezade's tales, are a thousand and one;
You remember the story,—those mornings in bed,—
'T was the turn of a copper,—a tale or a head.

A doom like Scheherezade's falls upon me
In a mandate as stern as the Sultan's decree
I'm a florist in verse, and what would people say
If I came to a banquet without my bouquet?

It is trying, no doubt, when the company knows
Just the look and the smell of each lily and rose,
The green of each leaf in the sprigs that I bring,
And the shape of the bunch and the knot of the string.

Yes,—"the style is the man," and the nib of one's pen
Makes the same mark at twenty, and threescore and ten;
It is so in all matters, if truth may be told;
Let one look at the cast he can tell you the mould.

How we all know each other! no use in disguise;
Through the holes in the mask comes the flash of the eyes;
We can tell by his—somewhat—each one of our tribe,
As we know the old hat which we cannot describe.

Though in Hebrew, in Sanscrit, in Choctaw you write,
Sweet singer who gave us the Voices of Night,
Though in buskin or slipper your song may be shod;
Or the velvety verse that Evangeline trod,

We shall say, "You can't cheat us,—we know it is you,"
There is one voice like that, but there cannot be two,
Maestro, whose chant like the dulcimer rings
And the woods will be hushed while the nightingale sings.

And he, so serene, so majestic, so true,
Whose temple hypethral the planets shine through,
Let us catch but five words from that mystical pen,
We should know our one sage from all children of men.

And he whose bright image no distance can dim,
Through a hundred disguises we can't mistake him,
Whose play is all earnest, whose wit is the edge
(With a beetle behind) of a sham-splitting wedge.

Do you know whom we send you, Hidalgos of Spain?
Do you know your old friends when you see them again?
Hosea was Sancho! you Dons of Madrid,
But Sancho that wielded the lance of the Cid!

And the wood-thrush of Essex,—you know whom I mean,
Whose song echoes round us while he sits unseen,
Whose heart-throbs of verse through our memories thrill
Like a breath from the wood, like a breeze from the hill,

So fervid, so simple, so loving, so pure,
We hear but one strain and our verdict is sure,—
Thee cannot elude us,—no further we search,—
'T is Holy George Herbert cut loose from his church!

We think it the voice of a seraph that sings,—
Alas! we remember that angels have wings,—
What story is this of the day of his birth?
Let him live to a hundred! we want him on earth!

One life has been paid him (in gold) by the sun;
One account has been squared and another begun;
But he never will die if he lingers below
Till we've paid him in love half the balance we owe!

TWO SONNETS: HARVARD

At the meeting of the New York Harvard Club,
February 21, 1878.

"CHRISTO ET ECCLESLE." 1700

To GOD'S ANOINTED AND HIS CHOSEN FLOCK
So ran the phrase the black-robed conclave chose
To guard the sacred cloisters that arose
Like David's altar on Moriah's rock.
Unshaken still those ancient arches mock
The ram's-horn summons of the windy foes
Who stand like Joshua's army while it blows
And wait to see them toppling with the shock.
Christ and the Church. Their church, whose narrow door
Shut out the many, who if overbold
Like hunted wolves were driven from the fold,
Bruised with the flails these godly zealots bore,
Mindful that Israel's altar stood of old
Where echoed once Araunah's threshing-floor.

1643 "VERITAS." 1878

TRUTH: So the frontlet's older legend ran,
On the brief record's opening page displayed;
Not yet those clear-eyed scholars were afraid
Lest the fair fruit that wrought the woe of man
By far Euphrates—where our sire began
His search for truth, and, seeking, was betrayed—

Might work new treason in their forest shade,
Doubling the curse that brought life's shortened span.
Nurse of the future, daughter of the past,
That stern phylactery best becomes thee now
Lift to the morning star thy marble brow
Cast thy brave truth on every warring blast!
Stretch thy white hand to that forbidden bough,
And let thine earliest symbol be thy last!

THE COMING ERA

THEY tell us that the Muse is soon to fly hence,
Leaving the bowers of song that once were dear,
Her robes bequeathing to her sister, Science,
The groves of Pindus for the axe to clear.

Optics will claim the wandering eye of fancy,
Physics will grasp imagination's wings,
Plain fact exorcise fiction's necromancy,
The workshop hammer where the minstrel sings,

No more with laugher at Thalia's frolics
Our eyes shall twinkle till the tears run down,
But in her place the lecturer on hydraulics
Spout forth his watery science to the town.

No more our foolish passions and affections
The tragic Muse with mimic grief shall try,
But, nobler far, a course of vivisections
Teach what it costs a tortured brute to die.

The unearthed monad, long in buried rocks hid,
Shall tell the secret whence our being came;
The chemist show us death is life's black oxide,
Left when the breath no longer fans its flame.

Instead of crack-brained poets in their attics
Filling thin volumes with their flowery talk,
There shall be books of wholesome mathematics;
The tutor with his blackboard and his chalk.

No longer bards with madrigal and sonnet
Shall woo to moonlight walks the ribboned sex,
But side by side the beaver and the bonnet
Stroll, calmly pondering on some problem's x.

The sober bliss of serious calculation
Shall mock the trivial joys that fancy drew,

And, oh, the rapture of a solved equation, —
One self-same answer on the lips of two!

So speak in solemn tones our youthful sages,
Patient, severe, laborious, slow, exact,
As o'er creation's protoplasmic pages
They browse and munch the thistle crops of fact.

And yet we 've sometimes found it rather pleasant
To dream again the scenes that Shakespeare drew, —
To walk the hill-side with the Scottish peasant
Among the daisies wet with morning's dew;

To leave awhile the daylight of the real,
Led by the guidance of the master's hand,
For the strange radiance of the far ideal, —
"The light that never was on sea or land."

Well, Time alone can lift the future's curtain, —
Science may teach our children all she knows,
But Love will kindle fresh young hearts, 't is certain,
And June will not forget her blushing rose.

And so, in spite of all that Time is bringing, —
Treasures of truth and miracles of art,
Beauty and Love will keep the poet singing,
And song still live, the science of the heart.

IN RESPONSE

Breakfast at the Century Club, New York, May, 1879.

SUCH kindness! the scowl of a cynic would soften,
His pulse beat its way to some eloquent words,
Alas! my poor accents have echoed too often,
Like that Pinafore music you've some of you heard.

Do you know me, dear strangers—the hundredth time comer
At banquets and feasts since the days of my Spring?
Ah! would I could borrow one rose of my Summer,
But this is a leaf of my Autumn I bring.

I look at your faces,—I'm sure there are some from
The three-breasted mother I count as my own;
You think you remember the place you have come from,
But how it has changed in the years that have flown!

Unaltered, 't is true, is the hall we call "Funnel,"
Still fights the "Old South" in the battle for life,
But we've opened our door to the West through the tunnel,
And we've cut off Fort Hill with our Amazon knife.

You should see the new Westminster Boston has builded,—
Its mansions, its spires, its museums of arts,—
You should see the great dome we have gorgeously gilded,—
'T is the light of our eyes, 't is the joy of our hearts.

When first in his path a young asteroid found it,
As he sailed through the skies with the stars in his wake,
He thought 't was the sun, and kept circling around it
Till Edison signalled, "You've made a mistake."

We are proud of our city,—her fast-growing figure,
The warp and the woof of her brain and her hands,—
But we're proudest of all that her heart has grown bigger,
And warms with fresh blood as her girdle expands.

One lesson the rubric of conflict has taught her
Though parted awhile by war's earth-rending shock,

The lines that divide us are written in water,
The love that unites us cut deep in the rock.

As well might the Judas of treason endeavor
To write his black name on the disk of the sun
As try the bright star-wreath that binds us to sever
And blot the fair legend of "Many in One."

We love You, tall sister, the stately, the splendid, —
The banner of empire floats high on your towers,
Yet ever in welcome your arms are extended, —
We share in your splendors, your glory is ours.

Yes, Queen of the Continent! All of us own thee, —
The gold-freighted argosies flock at thy call,
The naiads, the sea-nymphs have met to enthrone thee,
But the Broadway of one is the Highway of all!

I thank you. Three words that can hardly be mended,
Though phrases on phrases their eloquence pile,
If you hear the heart's throb with their eloquence blended,
And read all they mean in a sunshiny smile.

FOR THE MOORE CENTENNIAL CELEBRATION

MAY 28, 1879.

ENCHANTER of Erin, whose magic has bound us,
Thy wand for one moment we fondly would claim,
Entranced while it summons the phantoms around us
That blush into life at the sound of thy name.

The tell-tales of memory wake from their slumbers,—
I hear the old song with its tender refrain,—
What passion lies hid in those honey-voiced numbers
What perfume of youth in each exquisite strain!

The home of my childhood comes back as a vision,—
Hark! Hark! A soft chord from its song-haunted room,—
'T is a morning of May, when the air is Elysian,—
The syringa in bud and the lilac in bloom,—

We are clustered around the "Clementi" piano,—
There were six of us then,—there are two of us now,—
She is singing—the girl with the silver soprano—
How "The Lord of the Valley" was false to his vow;

"Let Erin remember" the echoes are calling;
Through "The Vale of Avoca" the waters are rolled;
"The Exile" laments while the night-dews falling;
"The Morning of Life" dawns again as of old.

But ah! those warm love-songs of fresh adolescence!
Around us such raptures celestial they flung
That it seemed as if Paradise breathed its quintessence
Through the seraph-toned lips of the maiden that sung!

Long hushed are the chords that my boyhood enchanted
As when the smooth wave by the angel was stirred,
Yet still with their music is memory haunted,
And oft in my dreams are their melodies heard.

I feel like the priest to his altar returning,—
The crowd that was kneeling no longer is there,

The flame has died down, but the brands are still burning,
And sandal and cinnamon sweeten the air.

II.

The veil for her bridal young Summer is weaving
In her azure-domed hall with its tapestried floor,
And Spring the last tear-drop of May-dew is leaving
On the daisy of Burns and the shamrock of Moore.

How like, how unlike, as we view them together,
The song of the minstrels whose record we scan, —
One fresh as the breeze blowing over the heather,
One sweet as the breath from an odalisque's fan!

Ah, passion can glow mid a palace's splendor;
The cage does not alter the song of the bird;
And the curtain of silk has known whispers as tender
As ever the blossoming hawthorn has heard.

No fear lest the step of the soft-slippered Graces
Should fright the young Loves from their warm little nest,
For the heart of a queen, under jewels and laces,
Beats time with the pulse in the peasant girl's breast!

Thrice welcome each gift of kind Nature's bestowing!
Her fountain heeds little the goblet we hold;
Alike, when its musical waters are flowing,
The shell from the seaside, the chalice of gold.

The twins of the lyre to her voices had listened;
Both laid their best gifts upon Liberty's shrine;
For Coila's loved minstrel the holly-wreath glistened;
For Erin's the rose and the myrtle entwine.

And while the fresh blossoms of summer are braided
For the sea-girdled, stream-silvered, lake-jewelled isle,
While her mantle of verdure is woven unfaded,
While Shannon and Liffey shall dimple and smile,

The land where the staff of Saint Patrick was planted,
Where the shamrock grows green from the cliffs to the shore,
The land of fair maidens and heroes undaunted,
Shall wreathe her bright harp with the garlands of Moore!

TO JAMES FREEMAN CLARKE

I BRING the simplest pledge of love,
Friend of my earlier days;
Mine is the hand without the glove,
The heart-beat, not the phrase.

How few still breathe this mortal air
We called by school-boy names!
You still, whatever robe you wear,
To me are always James.

That name the kind apostle bore
Who shames the sullen creeds,
Not trusting less, but loving more,
And showing faith by deeds.

What blending thoughts our memories share!
What visions yours and mine
Of May-days in whose morning air
The dews were golden wine,

Of vistas bright with opening day,
Whose all-awakening sun
Showed in life's landscape, far away,
The summits to be won!

The heights are gained. Ah, say not so
For him who smiles at time,
Leaves his tired comrades down below,
And only lives to climb!

His labors, — will they ever cease, —
With hand and tongue and pen?
Shall wearied Nature ask release
At threescore years and ten?

Our strength the clustered seasons tax, —
For him new life they mean;

Like rods around the lictor's axe
They keep him bright and keen.

  The wise, the brave, the strong, we know,—
We mark them here or there,
But he,—we roll our eyes, and lo!
We find him everywhere!

  With truth's bold cohorts, or alone,
He strides through error's field;
His lance is ever manhood's own,
His breast is woman's shield.

  Count not his years while earth has need
Of souls that Heaven inflames
With sacred zeal to save, to lead,—
Long live our dear Saint James!

WELCOME TO THE CHICAGO COMMERCIAL CLUB

January 14, 1880

CHICAGO sounds rough to the maker of verse;
One comfort we have—Cincinnati sounds worse;
If we only were licensed to say Chicago!
But Worcester and Webster won't let us, you know.

No matter, we songsters must sing as we can;
We can make some nice couplets with Lake Michigan,
And what more resembles a nightingale's voice,
Than the oily trisyllable, sweet Illinois?

Your waters are fresh, while our harbor is salt,
But we know you can't help it—it is n't your fault;
Our city is old and your city is new,
But the railroad men tell us we're greener than you.

You have seen our gilt dome, and no doubt you've been told
That the orbs of the universe round it are rolled;
But I'll own it to you, and I ought to know best,
That this is n't quite true of all stars of the West.

You'll go to Mount Auburn,—we'll show you the track,—
And can stay there,—unless you prefer to come back;
And Bunker's tall shaft you can climb if you will,
But you'll puff like a paragraph praising a pill.

You must see—but you have seen—our old Faneuil Hall,
Our churches, our school-rooms, our sample-rooms, all;
And, perhaps, though the idiots must have their jokes,
You have found our good people much like other folks.

There are cities by rivers, by lakes, and by seas,
Each as full of itself as a cheese-mite of cheese;
And a city will brag as a game-cock will crow
Don't your cockerels at home—just a little, you know?

But we'll crow for you now—here's a health to the boys,
Men, maidens, and matrons of fair Illinois,
And the rainbow of friendship that arches its span
From the green of the sea to the blue Michigan!

AMERICAN ACADEMY
CENTENNIAL CELEBRATION

MAY 26, 1880

SIRE, son, and grandson; so the century glides;
Three lives, three strides, three foot-prints in the sand;
Silent as midnight's falling meteor slides
Into the stillness of the far-off land;
How dim the space its little arc has spanned!

See on this opening page the names renowned
Tombed in these records on our dusty shelves,
Scarce on the scroll of living memory found,
Save where the wan-eyed antiquarian delves;
Shadows they seem; ab, what are we ourselves?

Pale ghosts of Bowdoin, Winthrop, Willard, West,
Sages of busy brain and wrinkled brow,
Searchers of Nature's secrets unconfessed,
Asking of all things Whence and Why and How —
What problems meet your larger vision now?

Has Gannett tracked the wild Aurora's path?
Has Bowdoin found his all-surrounding sphere?
What question puzzles ciphering Philomath?
Could Williams make the hidden causes clear
Of the Dark Day that filled the land with fear?

Dear ancient school-boys! Nature taught to them
The simple lessons of the star and flower,
Showed them strange sights; how on a single stem, —
Admire the marvels of Creative Power! —
Twin apples grew, one sweet, the other sour;

How from the hill-top where our eyes beheld
In even ranks the plumed and bannered maize
Range its long columns, in the days of old
The live volcano shot its angry blaze,—
Dead since the showers of Noah's watery days;

How, when the lightning split the mighty rock,
The spreading fury of the shaft was spent!
How the young scion joined the alien stock,
And when and where the homeless swallows went
To pass the winter of their discontent.

Scant were the gleanings in those years of dearth;
No Cuvier yet had clothed the fossil bones
That slumbered, waiting for their second birth;
No Lyell read the legend of the stones;
Science still pointed to her empty thrones.

Dreaming of orbs to eyes of earth unknown,
Herschel looked heavenwards in the starlight pale;
Lost in those awful depths he trod alone,
Laplace stood mute before the lifted veil;
While home-bred Humboldt trimmed his toy ship's sail.

No mortal feet these loftier heights had gained
Whence the wide realms of Nature we descry;
In vain their eyes our longing fathers strained
To scan with wondering gaze the summits high
That far beneath their children's footpaths lie.

Smile at their first small ventures as we may,
The school-boy's copy shapes the scholar's hand;
Their grateful memory fills our hearts to-day;
Brave, hopeful, wise, this bower of peace they planned,
While war's dread ploughshare scarred the suffering land.

Child of our children's children yet unborn,
When on this yellow page you turn your eyes,
Where the brief record of this May-day morn
In phrase antique and faded letters lies,
How vague, how pale our flitting ghosts will rise!

Yet in our veins the blood ran warm and red,
For us the fields were green, the skies were blue,
Though from our dust the spirit long has fled,
We lived, we loved, we toiled, we dreamed like you,
Smiled at our sires and thought how much we knew.

Oh might our spirits for one hour return,
When the next century rounds its hundredth ring,
All the strange secrets it shall teach to learn,
To hear the larger truths its years shall bring,
Its wiser sages talk, its sweeter minstrels sing!

THE SCHOOL-BOY

Read at the Centennial Celebration of the
foundation of Phillips Academy, Andover.

1778-1878

THESE hallowed precincts, long to memory dear,
Smile with fresh welcome as our feet draw near;
With softer gales the opening leaves are fanned,
With fairer hues the kindling flowers expand,
The rose-bush reddens with the blush of June,
The groves are vocal with their minstrels' tune,
The mighty elm, beneath whose arching shade
The wandering children of the forest strayed,
Greets the bright morning in its bridal dress,
And spreads its arms the gladsome dawn to bless.
Is it an idle dream that nature shares
Our joys, our griefs, our pastimes, and our cares?
Is there no summons when, at morning's call,
The sable vestments of the darkness fall?
Does not meek evening's low-voiced Ave blend
With the soft vesper as its notes ascend?
Is there no whisper in the perfumed air
When the sweet bosom of the rose is bare?
Does not the sunshine call us to rejoice?
Is there no meaning in the storm-cloud's voice?
No silent message when from midnight skies
Heaven looks upon us with its myriad eyes?

Or shift the mirror; say our dreams diffuse
O'er life's pale landscape their celestial hues,
Lend heaven the rainbow it has never known,
And robe the earth in glories not its own,
Sing their own music in the summer breeze,
With fresher foliage clothe the stately trees,
Stain the June blossoms with a livelier dye
And spread a bluer azure on the sky, —

Blest be the power that works its lawless will
And finds the weediest patch an Eden still;
No walls so fair as those our fancies build, —
No views so bright as those our visions gild!

So ran my lines, as pen and paper met,
The truant goose-quill travelling like Planchette;
Too ready servant, whose deceitful ways
Full many a slipshod line, alas! betrays;
Hence of the rhyming thousand not a few
Have builded worse—a great deal—than they knew.

What need of idle fancy to adorn
Our mother's birthplace on her birthday morn?
Hers are the blossoms of eternal spring,
From these green boughs her new-fledged birds take wing,
These echoes hear their earliest carols sung,
In this old nest the brood is ever young.
If some tired wanderer, resting from his flight,
Amid the gay young choristers alight,
These gather round him, mark his faded plumes
That faintly still the far-off grove perfumes,
And listen, wondering if some feeble note
Yet lingers, quavering in his weary throat:—
I, whose fresh voice yon red-faced temple knew,
What tune is left me, fit to sing to you?
Ask not the grandeurs of a labored song,
But let my easy couplets slide along;
Much could I tell you that you know too well;
Much I remember, but I will not tell;
Age brings experience; graybeards oft are wise,
But oh! how sharp a youngster's ears and eyes!

My cheek was bare of adolescent down
When first I sought the academic town;
Slow rolls the coach along the dusty road,
Big with its filial and parental load;
The frequent hills, the lonely woods are past,
The school-boy's chosen home is reached at last.
I see it now, the same unchanging spot,
The swinging gate, the little garden plot,
The narrow yard, the rock that made its floor,
The flat, pale house, the knocker-garnished door,
The small, trim parlor, neat, decorous, chill,

The strange, new faces, kind, but grave and still;
Two, creased with age,—or what I then called age,—
Life's volume open at its fiftieth page;
One, a shy maiden's, pallid, placid, sweet
As the first snow-drop, which the sunbeams greet;
One, the last nursling's; slight she was, and fair,
Her smooth white forehead warmed with auburn hair;
Last came the virgin Hymen long had spared,
Whose daily cares the grateful household shared,
Strong, patient, humble; her substantial frame
Stretched the chaste draperies I forbear to name.
Brave, but with effort, had the school-boy come
To the cold comfort of a stranger's home;
How like a dagger to my sinking heart
Came the dry summons, "It is time to part;
Good-by!" "Goo-ood-by!" one fond maternal kiss. . . .
Homesick as death! Was ever pang like this?
Too young as yet with willing feet to stray
From the tame fireside, glad to get away,—
Too old to let my watery grief appear,—
And what so bitter as a swallowed tear!
One figure still my vagrant thoughts pursue;
First boy to greet me, Ariel, where are you?
Imp of all mischief, heaven alone knows how
You learned it all,—are you an angel now,
Or tottering gently down the slope of years,
Your face grown sober in the vale of tears?
Forgive my freedom if you are breathing still;

    If in a happier world, I know you will.
You were a school-boy—what beneath the sun
So like a monkey? I was also one.
Strange, sure enough, to see what curious shoots
The nursery raises from the study's roots!
In those old days the very, very good
Took up more room—a little—than they should;
Something too much one's eyes encountered then
Of serious youth and funeral-visaged men;
The solemn elders saw life's mournful half,—
Heaven sent this boy, whose mission was to laugh,
Drollest of buffos, Nature's odd protest,
A catbird squealing in a blackbird's nest.

Kind, faithful Nature! While the sour-eyed Scot—
Her cheerful smiles forbidden or forgot—
Talks only of his preacher and his kirk,—
Hears five-hour sermons for his Sunday work,—
Praying and fasting till his meagre face
Gains its due length, the genuine sign of grace,—
An Ayrshire mother in the land of Knox
Her embryo poet in his cradle rocks;—
Nature, long shivering in her dim eclipse,
Steals in a sunbeam to those baby lips;
So to its home her banished smile returns,
And Scotland sweetens with the song of Burns!

  The morning came; I reached the classic hall;
A clock-face eyed me, staring from the wall;
Beneath its hands a printed line I read
YOUTH IS LIFE'S SEED-TIME: so the clock-face said:
Some took its counsel, as the sequel showed,—
Sowed,—their wild oats,—and reaped as they had sowed.
How all comes back! the upward slanting floor,—
The masters' thrones that flank the central door,—
The long, outstretching alleys that divide
The rows of desks that stand on either side,—
The staring boys, a face to every desk,
Bright, dull, pale, blooming, common, picturesque.
Grave is the Master's look; his forehead wears
Thick rows of wrinkles, prints of worrying cares;
Uneasy lie the heads of all that rule,
His most of all whose kingdom is a school.
Supreme he sits; before the awful frown
That bends his brows the boldest eye goes down;
Not more submissive Israel heard and saw
At Sinai's foot the Giver of the Law.
Less stern he seems, who sits in equal Mate
On the twin throne and shares the empire's weight;
Around his lips the subtle life that plays
Steals quaintly forth in many a jesting phrase;
A lightsome nature, not so hard to chafe,
Pleasant when pleased; rough-handled, not so safe;
Some tingling memories vaguely I recall,
But to forgive him. God forgive us all!

One yet remains, whose well-remembered name
Pleads in my grateful heart its tender claim;
His was the charm magnetic, the bright look
That sheds its sunshine on the dreariest book;
A loving soul to every task he brought
That sweetly mingled with the lore he taught;
Sprung from a saintly race that never could
From youth to age be anything but good,
His few brief years in holiest labors spent,
Earth lost too soon the treasure heaven had lent.
Kindest of teachers, studious to divine
Some hint of promise in my earliest line,
These faint and faltering words thou canst not hear
Throb from a heart that holds thy memory dear.
As to the traveller's eye the varied plain
Shows through the window of the flying train,
A mingled landscape, rather felt than seen,
A gravelly bank, a sudden flash of green,
A tangled wood, a glittering stream that flows
Through the cleft summit where the cliff once rose,
All strangely blended in a hurried gleam,
Rock, wood, waste, meadow, village, hill-side, stream, —
So, as we look behind us, life appears,
Seen through the vista of our bygone years.
Yet in the dead past's shadow-filled domain,
Some vanished shapes the hues of life retain;
Unbidden, oft, before our dreaming eyes
From the vague mists in memory's path they rise.
So comes his blooming image to my view,
The friend of joyous days when life was new,
Hope yet untamed, the blood of youth unchilled,
No blank arrear of promise unfulfilled,
Life's flower yet hidden in its sheltering fold,
Its pictured canvas yet to be unrolled.
His the frank smile I vainly look to greet,
His the warm grasp my clasping hand should meet;
How would our lips renew their school-boy talk,
Our feet retrace the old familiar walk!
For thee no more earth's cheerful morning shines
Through the green fringes of the tented pines;
Ah me! is heaven so far thou canst not hear,
Or is thy viewless spirit hovering near,

A fair young presence, bright with morning's glow,
The fresh-cheeked boy of fifty years ago?
Yes, fifty years, with all their circling suns,
Behind them all my glance reverted runs;
Where now that time remote, its griefs, its joys,
Where are its gray-haired men, its bright-haired boys?
Where is the patriarch time could hardly tire, —
The good old, wrinkled, immemorial "squire "?
(An honest treasurer, like a black-plumed swan,
Not every day our eyes may look upon.)
Where the tough champion who, with Calvin's sword,
In wordy conflicts battled for the Lord?
Where the grave scholar, lonely, calm, austere,
Whose voice like music charmed the listening ear,
Whose light rekindled, like the morning star
Still shines upon us through the gates ajar?
Where the still, solemn, weary, sad-eyed man,
Whose care-worn face and wandering eyes would scan, —
His features wasted in the lingering strife
With the pale foe that drains the student's life?
Where my old friend, the scholar, teacher, saint,
Whose creed, some hinted, showed a speck of taint;
He broached his own opinion, which is not
Lightly to be forgiven or forgot;
Some riddle's point, — I scarce remember now, —
Homoi-, perhaps, where they said homo-ou.
(If the unlettered greatly wish to know
Where lies the difference betwixt oi and o,
Those of the curious who have time may search
Among the stale conundrums of their church.)
Beneath his roof his peaceful life I shared,
And for his modes of faith I little cared, —
I, taught to judge men's dogmas by their deeds,
Long ere the days of india-rubber creeds.

Why should we look one common faith to find,
Where one in every score is color-blind?
If here on earth they know not red from green,
Will they see better into things unseen!
Once more to time's old graveyard I return
And scrape the moss from memory's pictured urn.
Who, in these days when all things go by steam,

Recalls the stage-coach with its four-horse team?
Its sturdy driver,—who remembers him?
Or the old landlord, saturnine and grim,
Who left our hill-top for a new abode
And reared his sign-post farther down the road?
Still in the waters of the dark Shawshine
Do the young bathers splash and think they're clean?
Do pilgrims find their way to Indian Ridge,
Or journey onward to the far-off bridge,
And bring to younger ears the story back
Of the broad stream, the mighty Merrimac?
Are there still truant feet that stray beyond
These circling bounds to Pomp's or Haggett's Pond,
Or where the legendary name recalls
The forest's earlier tenant,—"Deerjump Falls"?
Yes, every nook these youthful feet explore,
Just as our sires and grand sires did of yore;
So all life's opening paths, where nature led
Their father's feet, the children's children tread.
Roll the round century's fivescore years away,
Call from our storied past that earliest day
When great Eliphalet (I can see him now,—
Big name, big frame, big voice, and beetling brow),
Then young Eliphalet,—ruled the rows of boys
In homespun gray or old-world corduroys,—
And save for fashion's whims, the benches show
The self-same youths, the very boys we know.
Time works strange marvels: since I trod the green
And swung the gates, what wonders I have seen!
But come what will,—the sky itself may fall,—
As things of course the boy accepts them all.
The prophet's chariot, drawn by steeds of flame,
For daily use our travelling millions claim;
The face we love a sunbeam makes our own;
No more the surgeon hears the sufferer's groan;
What unwrit histories wrapped in darkness lay
Till shovelling Schliemann bared them to the day!
Your Richelieu says, and says it well, my lord,
The pen is (sometimes) mightier than the sword;
Great is the goosequill, say we all; Amen!
Sometimes the spade is mightier than the pen;
It shows where Babel's terraced walls were raised,

The slabs that cracked when Nimrod's palace blazed,
Unearths Mycenee, rediscovers Troy,—
Calmly he listens, that immortal boy.
A new Prometheus tips our wands with fire,
A mightier Orpheus strains the whispering wire,
Whose lightning thrills the lazy winds outrun
And hold the hours as Joshua stayed the sun,—
So swift, in truth, we hardly find a place
For those dim fictions known as time and space.
Still a new miracle each year supplies,—
See at his work the chemist of the skies,
Who questions Sirius in his tortured rays
And steals the secret of the solar blaze;
Hush! while the window-rattling bugles play
The nation's airs a hundred miles away!
That wicked phonograph! hark! how it swears!
Turn it again and make it say its prayers!
And was it true, then, what the story said
Of Oxford's friar and his brazen head?
While wondering Science stands, herself perplexed
At each day's miracle, and asks "What next?"
The immortal boy, the coming heir of all,
Springs from his desk to "urge the flying ball,"
Cleaves with his bending oar the glassy waves,
With sinewy arm the dashing current braves,
The same bright creature in these haunts of ours
That Eton shadowed with her "antique towers."

Boy! Where is he? the long-limbed youth inquires,
Whom his rough chin with manly pride inspires;
Ah, when the ruddy cheek no longer glows,
When the bright hair is white as winter snows,
When the dim eye has lost its lambent flame,
Sweet to his ear will be his school-boy name
Nor think the difference mighty as it seems
Between life's morning and its evening dreams;
Fourscore, like twenty, has its tasks and toys;
In earth's wide school-house all are girls and boys.

Brothers, forgive my wayward fancy. Who
Can guess beforehand what his pen will do?
Too light my strain for listeners such as these,
Whom graver thoughts and soberer speech shall please.

Is he not here whose breath of holy song
Has raised the downcast eyes of Faith so long?
Are they not here, the strangers in your gates,
For whom the wearied ear impatient waits, —
The large-brained scholars whom their toils release, —
The bannered heralds of the Prince of Peace?

Such was the gentle friend whose youth unblamed
In years long past our student-benches claimed;
Whose name, illumined on the sacred page,
Lives in the labors of his riper age;
Such he whose record time's destroying march
Leaves uneffaced on Zion's springing arch
Not to the scanty phrase of measured song,
Cramped in its fetters, names like these belong;
One ray they lend to gild my slender line, —
Their praise I leave to sweeter lips than mine.

Homes of our sires, where Learning's temple rose,
While yet they struggled with their banded foes,
As in the West thy century's sun descends,
One parting gleam its dying radiance lends.
Darker and deeper though the shadows fall
From the gray towers on Doubting Castle's wall,
Though Pope and Pagan re-array their hosts,
And her new armor youthful Science boasts,
Truth, for whose altar rose this holy shrine,
Shall fly for refuge to these bowers of thine;
No past shall chain her with its rusted vow,
No Jew's phylactery bind her Christian brow,
But Faith shall smile to find her sister free,
And nobler manhood draw its life from thee.

Long as the arching skies above thee spread,
As on thy groves the dews of heaven are shed,
With currents widening still from year to year,
And deepening channels, calm, untroubled, clear,
Flow the twin streamlets from thy sacred hill—
Pieria's fount and Siloam's shaded rill!

THE SILENT MELODY

"BRING me my broken harp," he said;
"We both are wrecks,—but as ye will,—
Though all its ringing tones have fled,
Their echoes linger round it still;
It had some golden strings, I know,
But that was long—how long!—ago.

"I cannot see its tarnished gold,
I cannot hear its vanished tone,
Scarce can my trembling fingers hold
The pillared frame so long their own;
We both are wrecks,—a while ago
It had some silver strings, I know,

"But on them Time too long has played
The solemn strain that knows no change,
And where of old my fingers strayed
The chords they find are new and strange,—
Yes! iron strings,—I know,—I know,—
We both are wrecks of long ago.

"We both are wrecks,—a shattered pair,—
Strange to ourselves in time's disguise.
What say ye to the lovesick air
That brought the tears from Marian's eyes?
Ay! trust me,—under breasts of snow
Hearts could be melted long ago!

"Or will ye hear the storm-song's crash
That from his dreams the soldier woke,
And bade him face the lightning flash
When battle's cloud in thunder broke? . . .
Wrecks,—nought but wrecks!—the time was when
We two were worth a thousand men!"

And so the broken harp they bring
With pitying smiles that none could blame;

Alas! there's not a single string
Of all that filled the tarnished frame!
But see! like children overjoyed,
His fingers rambling through the void!

"I clasp thee! Ay . . . mine ancient lyre . . .
Nay, guide my wandering fingers. . . There
They love to dally with the wire
As Isaac played with Esau's hair.
Hush! ye shall hear the famous tune
That Marian called the Breath of June!"

And so they softly gather round
Rapt in his tuneful trance he seems
His fingers move: but not a sound!
A silence like the song of dreams. . . .
"There! ye have heard the air," he cries,
"That brought the tears from Marian's eyes!"

Ah, smile not at his fond conceit,
Nor deem his fancy wrought in vain;
To him the unreal sounds are sweet, —
No discord mars the silent strain
Scored on life's latest, starlit page —
The voiceless melody of age.

Sweet are the lips, of all that sing,
When Nature's music breathes unsought,
But never yet could voice or string
So truly shape our tenderest thought
As when by life's decaying fire
Our fingers sweep the stringless lyre!

OUR HOME—OUR COUNTRY

FOR THE SEMI-CENTENNIAL CELEBRATION OF THE SETTLEMENT OF CAMBRIDGE, MASS., DECEMBER 28, 1880

YOUR home was mine,—kind Nature's gift;
My love no years can chill;
In vain their flakes the storm-winds sift,
The snow-drop hides beneath the drift,
A living blossom still.

Mute are a hundred long-famed lyres,
Hushed all their golden strings;
One lay the coldest bosom fires,
One song, one only, never tires
While sweet-voiced memory sings.

No spot so lone but echo knows
That dear familiar strain;
In tropic isles, on arctic snows,
Through burning lips its music flows
And rings its fond refrain.

From Pisa's tower my straining sight
Roamed wandering leagues away,
When lo! a frigate's banner bright,
The starry blue, the red, the white,
In far Livorno's bay.

Hot leaps the life-blood from my heart,
Forth springs the sudden tear;
The ship that rocks by yonder mart
Is of my land, my life, a part,—
Home, home, sweet home, is here!

Fades from my view the sunlit scene,—
My vision spans the waves;
I see the elm-encircled green,
The tower,—the steeple,—and, between,
The field of ancient graves.

There runs the path my feet would tread
When first they learned to stray;

There stands the gambrel roof that spread
Its quaint old angles o'er my head
When first I saw the day.

The sounds that met my boyish ear
My inward sense salute, —
The woodnotes wild I loved to hear, —
The robin's challenge, sharp and clear, —
The breath of evening's flute.

The faces loved from cradle days, —
Unseen, alas, how long!
As fond remembrance round them plays,
Touched with its softening moonlight rays,
Through fancy's portal throng.

And see! as if the opening skies
Some angel form had spared
Us wingless mortals to surprise,
The little maid with light-blue eyes,
White necked and golden haired!

. . . .

So rose the picture full in view
I paint in feebler song;
Such power the seamless banner knew
Of red and white and starry blue
For exiles banished long.

Oh, boys, dear boys, who wait as men
To guard its heaven-bright folds,
Blest are the eyes that see again
That banner, seamless now, as then, —
The fairest earth beholds!

Sweet was the Tuscan air and soft
In that unfading hour,
And fancy leads my footsteps oft
Up the round galleries, high aloft
On Pisa's threatening tower.

And still in Memory's holiest shrine
I read with pride and joy,
"For me those stars of empire shine;
That empire's dearest home is mine;
I am a Cambridge boy!"

POEM

AT THE CENTENNIAL ANNIVERSARY DINNER OF THE MASSACHUSETTS MEDICAL SOCIETY, JUNE 8, 1881

THREE paths there be where Learning's favored sons,
Trained in the schools which hold her favored ones,
Follow their several stars with separate aim;
Each has its honors, each its special claim.
Bred in the fruitful cradle of the East,
First, as of oldest lineage, comes the Priest;
The Lawyer next, in wordy conflict strong,
Full armed to battle for the right,—or wrong;
Last, he whose calling finds its voice in deeds,
Frail Nature's helper in her sharpest needs.

Each has his gifts, his losses and his gains,
Each his own share of pleasures and of pains;
No life-long aim with steadfast eye pursued
Finds a smooth pathway all with roses strewed;
Trouble belongs to man of woman born,—
Tread where he may, his foot will find its thorn.

Of all the guests at life's perennial feast,
Who of her children sits above the Priest?
For him the broidered robe, the carven seat,
Pride at his beck, and beauty at his feet,
For him the incense fumes, the wine is poured,
Himself a God, adoring and adored!
His the first welcome when our hearts rejoice,
His in our dying ear the latest voice,
Font, altar, grave, his steps on all attend,
Our staff, our stay, our all but heavenly friend!

Where is the meddling hand that dares to probe
The secret grief beneath his sable robe?
How grave his port! how every gesture tells
Here truth abides, here peace forever dwells;

Vex not his lofty soul with comments vain;
Faith asks no questions; silence, ye profane!

Alas! too oft while all is calm without
The stormy spirit wars with endless doubt;
This is the mocking spectre, scarce concealed
Behind tradition's bruised and battered shield.
He sees the sleepless critic, age by age,
Scrawl his new readings on the hallowed page,
The wondrous deeds that priests and prophets saw
Dissolved in legend, crystallized in law,
And on the soil where saints and martyrs trod
Altars new builded to the Unknown God;
His shrines imperilled, his evangels torn, —
He dares not limp, but ah! how sharp his thorn!

Yet while God's herald questions as he reads
The outworn dogmas of his ancient creeds,
Drops from his ritual the exploded verse,
Blots from its page the Athanasian curse,
Though by the critic's dangerous art perplexed,
His holy life is Heaven's unquestioned text;
That shining guidance doubt can never mar, —
The pillar's flame, the light of Bethlehem's star!

Strong is the moral blister that will draw
Laid on the conscience of the Man of Law
Whom blindfold Justice lends her eyes to see
Truth in the scale that holds his promised fee.
What! Has not every lie its truthful side,
Its honest fraction, not to be denied?
Per contra, — ask the moralist, — in sooth
Has not a lie its share in every truth?
Then what forbids an honest man to try
To find the truth that lurks in every lie,
And just as fairly call on truth to yield
The lying fraction in its breast concealed?
So the worst rogue shall claim a ready friend
His modest virtues boldly to defend,
And he who shows the record of a saint
See himself blacker than the devil could paint.

What struggles to his captive soul belong
Who loves the right, yet combats for the wrong,

Who fights the battle he would fain refuse,
And wins, well knowing that he ought to lose,
Who speaks with glowing lips and look sincere
In spangled words that make the worse appear
The better reason; who, behind his mask,
Hides his true self and blushes at his task,—
What quips, what quillets cheat the inward scorn
That mocks such triumph? Has he not his thorn?

Yet stay thy judgment; were thy life the prize,
Thy death the forfeit, would thy cynic eyes
See fault in him who bravely dares defend
The cause forlorn, the wretch without a friend
Nay, though the rightful side is wisdom's choice,
Wrong has its rights and claims a champion's voice;
Let the strong arm be lifted for the weak,
For the dumb lips the fluent pleader speak;—
When with warm "rebel" blood our street was dyed
Who took, unawed, the hated hirelings' side?
No greener civic wreath can Adams claim,
No brighter page the youthful Quincy's name!

How blest is he who knows no meaner strife
Than Art's long battle with the foes of life!
No doubt assails him, doing still his best,
And trusting kindly Nature for the rest;
No mocking conscience tears the thin disguise
That wraps his breast, and tells him that he lies.
He comes: the languid sufferer lifts his head
And smiles a welcome from his weary bed;
He speaks: what music like the tones that tell,
"Past is the hour of danger,—all is well!"
How can he feel the petty stings of grief
Whose cheering presence always brings relief?
What ugly dreams can trouble his repose
Who yields himself to soothe another's woes?

Hour after hour the busy day has found
The good physician on his lonely round;
Mansion and hovel, low and lofty door,
He knows, his journeys every path explore,—
Where the cold blast has struck with deadly chill
The sturdy dweller on the storm-swept hill,
Where by the stagnant marsh the sickening gale

Has blanched the poisoned tenants of the vale,
Where crushed and maimed the bleeding victim lies,
Where madness raves, where melancholy sighs,
And where the solemn whisper tells too plain
That all his science, all his art, were vain.

How sweet his fireside when the day is done
And cares have vanished with the setting sun!
Evening at last its hour of respite brings
And on his couch his weary length he flings.
Soft be thy pillow, servant of mankind,
Lulled by an opiate Art could never find;
Sweet be thy slumber,—thou hast earned it well,—
Pleasant thy dreams! Clang! goes the midnight bell!

Darkness and storm! the home is far away
That waits his coming ere the break of day;
The snow-clad pines their wintry plumage toss,—
Doubtful the frozen stream his road must cross;
Deep lie the drifts, the slanted heaps have shut
The hardy woodman in his mountain hut,—
Why should thy softer frame the tempest brave?
Hast thou no life, no health, to lose or save?
Look! read the answer in his patient eyes,—
For him no other voice when suffering cries;
Deaf to the gale that all around him blows,
A feeble whisper calls him,—and he goes.

Or seek the crowded city,—summer's heat
Glares burning, blinding, in the narrow street,
Still, noisome, deadly, sleeps the envenomed air,
Unstirred the yellow flag that says "Beware!"
Tempt not thy fate,—one little moment's breath
Bears on its viewless wing the seeds of death;
Thou at whose door the gilded chariots stand,
Whose dear-bought skill unclasps the miser's hand,
Turn from thy fatal quest, nor cast away
That life so precious; let a meaner prey
Feed the destroyer's hunger; live to bless
Those happier homes that need thy care no less!

Smiling he listens; has he then a charm
Whose magic virtues peril can disarm?
No safeguard his; no amulet he wears,

Too well he knows that Nature never spares
Her truest servant, powerless to defend
From her own weapons her unshrinking friend.
He dares the fate the bravest well might shun,
Nor asks reward save only Heaven's "Well done!"

Such are the toils, the perils that he knows,
Days without rest and nights without repose,
Yet all unheeded for the love he bears
His art, his kind, whose every grief he shares.

Harder than these to know how small the part
Nature's proud empire yields to striving Art;
How, as the tide that rolls around the sphere
Laughs at the mounds that delving arms uprear,—
Spares some few roods of oozy earth, but still
Wastes and rebuilds the planet at its will,
Comes at its ordered season, night or noon,
Led by the silver magnet of the moon,—
So life's vast tide forever comes and goes,
Unchecked, resistless, as it ebbs and flows.

Hardest of all, when Art has done her best,
To find the cuckoo brooding in her nest;
The shrewd adventurer, fresh from parts unknown,
Kills off the patients Science thought her own;
Towns from a nostrum-vender get their name,
Fences and walls the cure-all drug proclaim,
Plasters and pads the willing world beguile,
Fair Lydia greets us with astringent smile,
Munchausen's fellow-countryman unlocks
His new Pandora's globule-holding box,
And as King George inquired, with puzzled grin,
"How—how the devil get the apple in?"
So we ask how,—with wonder-opening eyes,—
Such pygmy pills can hold such giant lies!

Yes, sharp the trials, stern the daily tasks
That suffering Nature from her servant asks;
His the kind office dainty menials scorn,
His path how hard,—at every step a thorn!
What does his saddening, restless slavery buy?
What save a right to live, a chance to die,—

To live companion of disease and pain,
To die by poisoned shafts untimely slain?

Answer from hoary eld, majestic shades, —
From Memphian courts, from Delphic colonnades,
Speak in the tones that Persia's despot heard
When nations treasured every golden word
The wandering echoes wafted o'er the seas,
From the far isle that held Hippocrates;
And thou, best gift that Pergamus could send
Imperial Rome, her noblest Caesar's friend,
Master of masters, whose unchallenged sway
Not bold Vesalius dared to disobey;
Ye who while prophets dreamed of dawning times
Taught your rude lessons in Salerno's rhymes,
And ye, the nearer sires, to whom we owe
The better share of all the best we know,
In every land an ever-growing train,
Since wakening Science broke her rusted chain, —
Speak from the past, and say what prize was sent
To crown the toiling years so freely spent!

List while they speak:
In life's uneven road
Our willing hands have eased our brothers' load;
One forehead smoothed, one pang of torture less,
One peaceful hour a sufferer's couch to bless,
The smile brought back to fever's parching lips,
The light restored to reason in eclipse,
Life's treasure rescued like a burning brand
Snatched from the dread destroyer's wasteful hand;
Such were our simple records day by day,
For gains like these we wore our lives away.
In toilsome paths our daily bread we sought,
But bread from heaven attending angels brought;
Pain was our teacher, speaking to the heart,
Mother of pity, nurse of pitying art;
Our lesson learned, we reached the peaceful shore
Where the pale sufferer asks our aid no more, —
These gracious words our welcome, our reward
Ye served your brothers; ye have served your Lord!

RHYMES OF A LIFE-TIME

FROM the first gleam of morning to the gray
Of peaceful evening, lo, a life unrolled!
In woven pictures all its changes told,
Its lights, its shadows, every flitting ray,
Till the long curtain, falling, dims the day,
Steals from the dial's disk the sunlight's gold,
And all the graven hours grow dark and cold
Where late the glowing blaze of noontide lay.
Ah! the warm blood runs wild in youthful veins,—
Let me no longer play with painted fire;
New songs for new-born days! I would not tire
The listening ears that wait for fresher strains
In phrase new-moulded, new-forged rhythmic chains,
With plaintive measures from a worn-out lyre.
August 2, 1881.

BEFORE THE CURFEW

AT MY FIRESIDE

ALONE, beneath the darkened sky,
With saddened heart and unstrung lyre,
I heap the spoils of years gone by,
And leave them with a long-drawn sigh,
Like drift-wood brands that glimmering lie,
Before the ashes hide the fire.

Let not these slow declining days
The rosy light of dawn outlast;
Still round my lonely hearth it plays,
And gilds the east with borrowed rays,
While memory's mirrored sunset blaze
Flames on the windows of the past.

March 1, 1888.

AT THE SATURDAY CLUB

THIS is our place of meeting; opposite
That towered and pillared building: look at it;
King's Chapel in the Second George's day,
Rebellion stole its regal name away, —
Stone Chapel sounded better; but at last
The poisoned name of our provincial past
Had lost its ancient venom; then once more
Stone Chapel was King's Chapel as before.
(So let rechristened North Street, when it can,
Bring back the days of Marlborough and Queen Anne!)
Next the old church your wandering eye will meet—
A granite pile that stares upon the street—
Our civic temple; slanderous tongues have said
Its shape was modelled from St. Botolph's head,
Lofty, but narrow; jealous passers-by
Say Boston always held her head too high.

Turn half-way round, and let your look survey
The white facade that gleams across the way,—
The many-windowed building, tall and wide,
The palace-inn that shows its northern side
In grateful shadow when the sunbeams beat
The granite wall in summer's scorching heat.
This is the place; whether its name you spell
Tavern, or caravansera, or hotel.
Would I could steal its echoes! you should find
Such store of vanished pleasures brought to mind
Such feasts! the laughs of many a jocund hour
That shook the mortar from King George's tower;
Such guests! What famous names its record boasts,
Whose owners wander in the mob of ghosts!
Such stories! Every beam and plank is filled
With juicy wit the joyous talkers spilled,
Ready to ooze, as once the mountain pine
The floors are laid with oozed its turpentine!

A month had flitted since The Club had met;
The day came round; I found the table set,
The waiters lounging round the marble stairs,
Empty as yet the double row of chairs.
I was a full half hour before the rest,
Alone, the banquet-chamber's single guest.
So from the table's side a chair I took,
And having neither company nor book
To keep me waking, by degrees there crept
A torpor over me,—in short, I slept.

Loosed from its chain, along the wreck-strown track
Of the dead years my soul goes travelling back;
My ghosts take on their robes of flesh; it seems
Dreaming is life; nay, life less life than dreams,
So real are the shapes that meet my eyes.
They bring no sense of wonder, no surprise,
No hint of other than an earth-born source;
All seems plain daylight, everything of course.

How dim the colors are, how poor and faint
This palette of weak words with which I paint!
Here sit my friends; if I could fix them so
As to my eyes they seem, my page would glow
Like a queen's missal, warm as if the brush

Of Titian or Velasquez brought the flush
Of life into their features. Ay de mi!
If syllables were pigments, you should see
Such breathing portraitures as never man
Found in the Pitti or the Vatican.

Here sits our POET, Laureate, if you will.
Long has he worn the wreath, and wears it still.
Dead? Nay, not so; and yet they say his bust
Looks down on marbles covering royal dust,
Kings by the Grace of God, or Nature's grace;
Dead! No! Alive! I see him in his place,
Full-featured, with the bloom that heaven denies
Her children, pinched by cold New England skies,
Too often, while the nursery's happier few
Win from a summer cloud its roseate hue.
Kind, soft-voiced, gentle, in his eye there shines
The ray serene that filled Evangeline's.
Modest he seems, not shy; content to wait
Amid the noisy clamor of debate
The looked-for moment when a peaceful word
Smooths the rough ripples louder tongues have stirred.
In every tone I mark his tender grace
And all his poems hinted in his face;
What tranquil joy his friendly presence gives!
How could. I think him dead? He lives! He lives!

There, at the table's further end I see
In his old place our Poet's vis-a-vis,
The great PROFESSOR, strong, broad-shouldered, square,
In life's rich noontide, joyous, debonair.
His social hour no leaden care alloys,
His laugh rings loud and mirthful as a boy's, —
That lusty laugh the Puritan forgot, —
What ear has heard it and remembers not?
How often, halting at some wide crevasse
Amid the windings of his Alpine pass,
High up the cliffs, the climbing mountaineer,
Listening the far-off avalanche to hear,
Silent, and leaning on his steel-shod staff,
Has heard that cheery voice, that ringing laugh,
From the rude cabin whose nomadic walls
Creep with the moving glacier as it crawls

How does vast Nature lead her living train
In ordered sequence through that spacious brain,
As in the primal hour when Adam named
The new-born tribes that young creation claimed! —
How will her realm be darkened, losing thee,
Her darling, whom we call *our* AGASSIZ!

But who is he whose massive frame belies
The maiden shyness of his downcast eyes?
Who broods in silence till, by questions pressed,
Some answer struggles from his laboring breast?
An artist Nature meant to dwell apart,
Locked in his studio with a human heart,
Tracking its eaverned passions to their lair,
And all its throbbing mysteries laying bare.
Count it no marvel that he broods alone
Over the heart he studies, — 't is his own;
So in his page, whatever shape it wear,
The Essex wizard's shadowed self is there, —
The great ROMANCER, hid beneath his veil
Like the stern preacher of his sombre tale;
Virile in strength, yet bashful as a girl,
Prouder than Hester, sensitive as Pearl.

From his mild throng of worshippers released,
Our Concord Delphi sends its chosen priest,
Prophet or poet, mystic, sage, or seer,
By every title always welcome here.
Why that ethereal spirit's frame describe?
You know the race-marks of the Brahmin tribe,
The spare, slight form, the sloping shoulders' droop,
The calm, scholastic mien, the clerkly stoop,
The lines of thought the sharpened features wear,
Carved by the edge of keen New England air.
List! for he speaks! As when a king would choose
The jewels for his bride, he might refuse
This diamond for its flaw, — find that less bright
Than those, its fellows, and a pearl less white
Than fits her snowy neck, and yet at last,
The fairest gems are chosen, and made fast
In golden fetters; so, with light delays
He seeks the fittest word to fill his phrase;
Nor vain nor idle his fastidious quest,

His chosen word is sure to prove the best.
Where in the realm of thought, whose air is song,
Does he, the Buddha of the West, belong?
He seems a winged Franklin, sweetly wise,
Born to unlock the secrets of the skies;
And which the nobler calling,—if 't is fair
Terrestrial with celestial to compare,—
To guide the storm-cloud's elemental flame,
Or walk the chambers whence the lightning came,
Amidst the sources of its subtile fire,
And steal their effluence for his lips and lyre?
If lost at times in vague aerial flights,
None treads with firmer footstep when he lights;
A soaring nature, ballasted with sense,
Wisdom without her wrinkles or pretence,
In every Bible he has faith to read,
And every altar helps to shape his creed.
Ask you what name this prisoned spirit bears
While with ourselves this fleeting breath it shares?
Till angels greet him with a sweeter one
In heaven, on earth we call him EMERSON.

    I start; I wake; the vision is withdrawn;
Its figures fading like the stars at dawn;
Crossed from the roll of life their cherished names,
And memory's pictures fading in their frames;
Yet life is lovelier for these transient gleams
Of buried friendships; blest is he who dreams!

OUR DEAD SINGER

H. W. L.

PRIDE of the sister realm so long our own,
We claim with her that spotless fame of thine,
White as her snow and fragrant as her pine!
Ours was thy birthplace, but in every zone
Some wreath of song thy liberal hand has thrown
Breathes perfume from its blossoms, that entwine
Where'er the dewdrops fall, the sunbeams shine,
On life's long path with tangled cares o'ergrown.
Can Art thy truthful counterfeit command,—
The silver-haloed features, tranquil, mild,—
Soften the lips of bronze as when they smiled,
Give warmth and pressure to the marble hand?
Seek the lost rainbow in the sky it spanned
Farewell, sweet Singer! Heaven reclaims its child.

Carved from the block or cast in clinging mould,
Will grateful Memory fondly try her best
The mortal vesture from decay to wrest;
His look shall greet us, calm, but ah, how cold!
No breath can stir the brazen drapery's fold,
No throb can heave the statue's stony breast;
"He is not here, but risen," will stand confest
In all we miss, in all our eyes behold.
How Nature loved him! On his placid brow,
Thought's ample dome, she set the sacred sign
That marks the priesthood of her holiest shrine,
Nor asked a leaflet from the laurel's bough
That envious Time might clutch or disallow,
To prove her chosen minstrel's song divine.

On many a saddened hearth the evening fire
Burns paler as the children's hour draws near,—
That joyous hour his song made doubly dear,—
And tender memories touch the faltering choir.

He sings no more on earth; our vain desire
Aches for the voice we loved so long to hear
In Dorian flute-notes breathing soft and clear, —
The sweet contralto that could never tire.
Deafened with listening to a harsher strain,
The Maenad's scream, the stark barbarian's cry,
Still for those soothing, loving tones we sigh;
Oh, for our vanished Orpheus once again!
The shadowy silence hears us call in vain!
His lips are hushed; his song shall never die.

TWO POEMS TO HARRIET BEECHER STOWE

ON HER SEVENTIETH BIRTHDAY, JUNE 14, 1882

I. AT THE SUMMIT

SISTER, we bid you welcome, — we who stand
On the high table-land;
We who have climbed life's slippery Alpine slope,
And rest, still leaning on the staff of hope,
Looking along the silent Mer de Glace,
Leading our footsteps where the dark crevasse
Yawns in the frozen sea we all must pass, —
Sister, we clasp your hand!

Rest with us in the hour that Heaven has lent
Before the swift descent.
Look! the warm sunbeams kiss the glittering ice;
See! next the snow-drift blooms the edelweiss;
The mated eagles fan the frosty air;
Life, beauty, love, around us everywhere,
And, in their time, the darkening hours that bear
Sweet memories, peace, content.

Thrice welcome! shining names our missals show
Amid their rubrics' glow,
But search the blazoned record's starry line,
What halo's radiance fills the page like thine?
Thou who by some celestial clue couldst find
The way to all the hearts of all mankind,
On thee, already canonized, enshrined,
What more can Heaven bestow!

II. THE WORLD'S HOMAGE

IF every tongue that speaks her praise
For whom I shape my tinkling phrase
Were summoned to the table,

The vocal chorus that would meet
Of mingling accents harsh or sweet,
From every land and tribe, would beat
The polyglots at Babel.

Briton and Frenchman, Swede and Dane,
Turk, Spaniard, Tartar of Ukraine,
Hidalgo, Cossack, Cadi,
High Dutchman and Low Dutchman, too,
The Russian serf, the Polish Jew,
Arab, Armenian, and Mantchoo,
Would shout, "We know the lady!"

Know her! Who knows not Uncle Tom
And her he learned his gospel from
Has never heard of Moses;
Full well the brave black hand we know
That gave to freedom's grasp the hoe
That killed the weed that used to grow
Among the Southern roses.

When Archimedes, long ago,
Spoke out so grandly, " *dos pou sto* —
Give me a place to stand on,
I'll move your planet for you, now," —
He little dreamed or fancied how
The *sto* at last should find its pou
For woman's faith to land on.

Her lever was the wand of art,
Her fulcrum was the human heart,
Whence all unfailing aid is;
She moved the earth! Its thunders pealed,
Its mountains shook, its temples reeled,
The blood-red fountains were unsealed,
And Moloch sunk to Hades.

All through the conflict, up and down
Marched Uncle Tom and Old John Brown,
One ghost, one form ideal;
And which was false and which was true,
And which was mightier of the two,

The wisest sibyl never knew,
For both alike were real.

Sister, the holy maid does well
Who counts her beads in convent cell,
Where pale devotion lingers;
But she who serves the sufferer's needs,
Whose prayers are spelt in loving deeds,
May trust the Lord will count her beads
As well as human fingers.

When Truth herself was Slavery's slave,
Thy hand the prisoned suppliant gave
The rainbow wings of fiction.
And Truth who soared descends to-day
Bearing an angel's wreath away,
Its lilies at thy feet to lay
With Heaven's own benediction.

A WELCOME TO DR. BENJAMIN APTHORP GOULD

ON HIS RETURN FROM SOUTH AMERICA

AFTER FIFTEEN YEARS DEVOTED TO CATALOGUING THE STARS OF THE SOUTHERN HEMISPHERE

Read at the Dinner given at the Hotel Vendome, May 6,1885.

ONCE more Orion and the sister Seven
Look on thee from the skies that hailed thy birth,—
How shall we welcome thee, whose home was heaven,
From thy celestial wanderings back to earth?

Science has kept her midnight taper burning
To greet thy coming with its vestal flame;
Friendship has murmured, "When art thou returning?"
"Not yet! Not yet!" the answering message came.

Thine was unstinted zeal, unchilled devotion,
While the blue realm had kingdoms to explore,—
Patience, like his who ploughed the unfurrowed ocean,
Till o'er its margin loomed San Salvador.

Through the long nights I see thee ever waking,
Thy footstool earth, thy roof the hemisphere,
While with thy griefs our weaker hearts are aching,
Firm as thine equatorial's rock-based pier.

The souls that voyaged the azure depths before thee
Watch with thy tireless vigils, all unseen,—
Tycho and Kepler bend benignant o'er thee,
And with his toy-like tube the Florentine,—

He at whose word the orb that bore him shivered
To find her central sovereignty disowned,

While the wan lips of priest and pontiff quivered,
Their jargon stilled, their Baal disenthroned.

Flamsteed and Newton look with brows unclouded,
Their strife forgotten with its faded scars, —
(Titans, who found the world of space too crowded
To walk in peace among its myriad stars.)

All cluster round thee, —seers of earliest ages,
Persians, Ionians, Mizraim's learned kings,
From the dim days of Shinar's hoary sages
To his who weighed the planet's fluid rings.

And we, for whom the northern heavens are lighted,
For whom the storm has passed, the sun has smiled,
Our clouds all scattered, all our stars united,
We claim thee, clasp thee, like a long-lost child.

Fresh from the spangled vault's o'er-arching splendor,
Thy lonely pillar, thy revolving dome,
In heartfelt accents, proud, rejoicing, tender,
We bid thee welcome to thine earthly home!

TO FREDERICK HENRY HEDGE

AT A DINNER GIVEN HIM ON HIS EIGHTIETH
BIRTHDAY, DECEMBER 12, 1885

With a bronze statuette of John of Bologna's
Mercury, presented by a few friends.

FIT emblem for the altar's side,
And him who serves its daily need,
The stay, the solace, and the guide
Of mortal men, whate'er his creed!

Flamen or Auspex, Priest or Bonze,
He feeds the upward-climbing fire,
Still teaching, like the deathless bronze,
Man's noblest lesson,—to aspire.

Hermes lies prone by fallen Jove,
Crushed are the wheels of Krishna's car,
And o'er Dodona's silent grove
Streams the white, ray from Bethlehem's star.

Yet snatched from Time's relentless clutch,
A godlike shape, that human hands
Have fired with Art's electric touch,
The herald of Olympus stands.

Ask not what ore the furnace knew;
Love mingled with the flowing mass,
And lends its own unchanging hue,
Like gold in Corinth's molten brass.

Take then our gift; this airy form
Whose bronze our benedictions gild,
The hearts of all its givers warm
With love by freezing years unchilled.

With eye undimmed, with strength unworn,
Still toiling in your Master's field,
Before you wave the growths unshorn,
Their ripened harvest yet to yield.

True servant of the Heavenly Sire,
To you our tried affection clings,
Bids you still labor, still aspire,
But clasps your feet and steals their wings.

TO JAMES RUSSELL LOWELL

THIS is your month, the month of "perfect days,"
Birds in full song and blossoms all ablaze.
Nature herself your earliest welcome breathes,
Spreads every leaflet, every bower inwreathes;
Carpets her paths for your returning feet,
Puts forth her best your coming steps to greet;
And Heaven must surely find the earth in tune
When Home, sweet Home, exhales the breath of June.
These blessed days are waning all too fast,
And June's bright visions mingling with the past;

Lilacs have bloomed and faded, and the rose
Has dropped its petals, but the clover blows,
And fills its slender tubes with honeyed sweets;
The fields are pearled with milk-white margarites;
The dandelion, which you sang of old,
Has lost its pride of place, its crown of gold,
But still displays its feathery-mantled globe,
Which children's breath, or wandering winds unrobe.
These were your humble friends; your opened eyes
Nature had trained her common gifts to prize;
Not Cam nor Isis taught you to despise
Charles, with his muddy margin and the harsh,
Plebeian grasses of the reeking marsh.
New England's home-bred scholar, well you knew
Her soil, her speech, her people, through and through,
And loved them ever with the love that holds
All sweet, fond memories in its fragrant folds.
Though far and wide your winged words have flown,
Your daily presence kept you all our own,
Till, with a sorrowing sigh, a thrill of pride,
We heard your summons, and you left our side
For larger duties and for tasks untried.

How pleased the Spaniards for a while to claim
This frank Hidalgo with the liquid name,
Who stored their classics on his crowded shelves
And loved their Calderon as they did themselves!
Before his eyes what changing pageants pass!
The bridal feast how near the funeral mass!
The death-stroke falls,—the Misereres wail;
The joy-bells ring,—the tear-stained cheeks unveil,
While, as the playwright shifts his pictured scene,
The royal mourner crowns his second queen.

From Spain to Britain is a goodly stride,—
Madrid and London long-stretched leagues divide.
What if I send him, "Uncle S., says he,"
To my good cousin whom he calls "J. B."?
A nation's servants go where they are sent,—
He heard his Uncle's orders, and he went.
By what enchantments, what alluring arts,
Our truthful James led captive British hearts,—
Whether his shrewdness made their statesmen halt,
Or if his learning found their Dons at fault,
Or if his virtue was a strange surprise,
Or if his wit flung star-dust in their eyes,—
Like honest Yankees we can simply guess;
But that he did it all must needs confess.
England herself without a blush may claim
Her only conqueror since the Norman came.
Eight years an exile! What a weary while
Since first our herald sought the mother isle!
His snow-white flag no churlish wrong has soiled,—-
He left unchallenged, he returns unspoiled.

Here let us keep him, here he saw the light,—
His genius, wisdom, wit, are ours by right;
And if we lose him our lament will be
We have "five hundred"— *not* "as good as he."

TO JOHN GREENLEAF WHITTIER

ON HIS EIGHTIETH BIRTHDAY

1887

FRIEND, whom thy fourscore winters leave more dear
Than when life's roseate summer on thy cheek
Burned in the flush of manhood's manliest year,
Lonely, how lonely! is the snowy peak
Thy feet have reached, and mine have climbed so near!
Close on thy footsteps 'mid the landscape drear
I stretch my hand thine answering grasp to seek,
Warm with the love no rippling rhymes can speak!
Look backward! From thy lofty height survey
Thy years of toil, of peaceful victories won,
Of dreams made real, largest hopes outrun!
Look forward! Brighter than earth's morning ray
Streams the pure light of Heaven's unsetting sun,
The unclouded dawn of life's immortal day!

PRELUDE TO A VOLUME PRINTED IN RAISED LETTERS FOR THE BLIND

DEAR friends, left darkling in the long eclipse
That veils the noonday,—you whose finger-tips
A meaning in these ridgy leaves can find
Where ours go stumbling, senseless, helpless, blind.
This wreath of verse how dare I offer you
To whom the garden's choicest gifts are due?
The hues of all its glowing beds are ours,
Shall you not claim its sweetest-smelling flowers?

Nay, those I have I bring you,—at their birth
Life's cheerful sunshine warmed the grateful earth;
If my rash boyhood dropped some idle seeds,
And here and there you light on saucy weeds
Among the fairer growths, remember still
Song comes of grace, and not of human will:
We get a jarring note when most we try,
Then strike the chord we know not how or why;
Our stately verse with too aspiring art
Oft overshoots and fails to reach the heart,
While the rude rhyme one human throb endears
Turns grief to smiles, and softens mirth to tears.
Kindest of critics, ye whose fingers read,
From Nature's lesson learn the poet's creed;
The queenly tulip flaunts in robes of flame,
The wayside seedling scarce a tint may claim,
Yet may the lowliest leaflets that unfold
A dewdrop fresh from heaven's own chalice hold.

BOSTON TO FLORENCE

Sent to "The Philological Circle" of Florence for
its meeting in commemoration of Dante, January 27,
1881, the anniversary of his first condemnation.

PROUD of her clustering spires, her new-built towers,
Our Venice, stolen from the slumbering sea,
A sister's kindliest greeting wafts to thee,
Rose of Val d' Arno, queen of all its flowers!
Thine exile's shrine thy sorrowing love embowers,
Yet none with truer homage bends the knee,
Or stronger pledge of fealty brings, than we,
Whose poets make thy dead Immortal ours.
Lonely the height, but ah, to heaven how near!
Dante, whence flowed that solemn verse of thine
Like the stern river from its Apennine
Whose name the far-off Scythian thrilled with fear:
Now to all lands thy deep-toned voice is dear,
And every language knows the Song Divine!

AT THE UNITARIAN FESTIVAL

MARCH 8, 1882

THE waves unbuild the wasting shore;
Where mountains towered the billows sweep,
Yet still their borrowed spoils restore,
And build new empires from the deep.
So while the floods of thought lay waste
The proud domain of priestly creeds,
Its heaven-appointed tides will haste
To plant new homes for human needs.
Be ours to mark with hearts unchilled
The change an outworn church deplores;
The legend sinks, but Faith shall build
A fairer throne on new-found shores.

POEM

FOR THE TWO HUNDRED AND FIFTIETH ANNIVERSARY OF THE FOUNDING OF HARVARD COLLEGE

TWICE had the mellowing sun of autumn crowned
The hundredth circle of his yearly round,
When, as we meet to-day, our fathers met:
That joyous gathering who can e'er forget,
When Harvard's nurslings, scattered far and wide,
Through mart and village, lake's and ocean's side,
Came, with one impulse, one fraternal throng,
And crowned the hours with banquet, speech, and song?

Once more revived in fancy's magic glass,
I see in state the long procession pass
Tall, courtly, leader as by right divine,
Winthrop, our Winthrop, rules the marshalled line,
Still seen in front, as on that far-off day
His ribboned baton showed the column's way.
Not all are gone who marched in manly pride
And waved their truncheons at their leader's side;
Gray, Lowell, Dixwell, who his empire shared,
These to be with us envious Time has spared.

Few are the faces, so familiar then,
Our eyes still meet amid the haunts of men;
Scarce one of all the living gathered there,
Whose unthinned locks betrayed a silver hair,
Greets us to-day, and yet we seem the same
As our own sires and grandsires, save in name.
There are the patriarchs, looking vaguely round
For classmates' faces, hardly known if found;
See the cold brow that rules the busy mart;
Close at its side the pallid son of art,
Whose purchased skill with borrowed meaning clothes,
And stolen hues, the smirking face he loathes.
Here is the patient scholar; in his looks

You read the titles of his learned books;
What classic lore those spidery crow's-feet speak!
What problems figure on that wrinkled cheek!
For never thought but left its stiffened trace,
Its fossil footprint, on the plastic face,
As the swift record of a raindrop stands,
Fixed on the tablet of the hardening sands.
On every face as on the written page
Each year renews the autograph of age;
One trait alone may wasting years defy, —
The fire still lingering in the poet's eye,
While Hope, the siren, sings her sweetest strain, —
Non omnis moriar is its proud refrain.

Sadly we gaze upon the vacant chair;
He who should claim its honors is not there, —
Otis, whose lips the listening crowd enthrall
That press and pack the floor of Boston's hall.
But Kirkland smiles, released from toil and care
Since the silk mantle younger shoulders wear, —
Quincy's, whose spirit breathes the selfsame fire
That filled the bosom of his youthful sire,
Who for the altar bore the kindled torch
To freedom's temple, dying in its porch.

Three grave professions in their sons appear,
Whose words well studied all well pleased will hear
Palfrey, ordained in varied walks to shine,
Statesman, historian, critic, and divine;
Solid and square behold majestic Shaw,
A mass of wisdom and a mine of law;
Warren, whose arm the doughtiest warriors fear,
Asks of the startled crowd to lend its ear, —
Proud of his calling, him the world loves best,
Not as the coming, but the parting guest.

Look on that form, — with eye dilating scan
The stately mould of nature's kingliest man!
Tower-like he stands in life's unfaded prime;
Ask you his name? None asks a second time
He from the land his outward semblance takes,
Where storm-swept mountains watch o'er slumbering lakes.
See in the impress which the body wears
How its imperial might the soul declares

The forehead's large expansion, lofty, wide,
That locks unsilvered vainly strive to hide;
The lines of thought that plough the sober cheek;
Lips that betray their wisdom ere they speak
In tones like answers from Dodona's grove;
An eye like Juno's when she frowns on Jove.
I look and wonder; will he be content—
This man, this monarch, for the purple meant—
The meaner duties of his tribe to share,
Clad in the garb that common mortals wear?
Ah, wild Ambition, spread thy restless wings,
Beneath whose plumes the hidden cestrum stings;

Thou whose bold flight would leave earth's vulgar crowds,
And like the eagle soar above the clouds,
Must feel the pang that fallen angels know
When the red lightning strikes thee from below!

Less bronze, more silver, mingles in the mould
Of him whom next my roving eyes behold;
His, more the scholar's than the statesman's face,
Proclaims him born of academic race.
Weary his look, as if an aching brain
Left on his brow the frozen prints of pain;
His voice far-reaching, grave, sonorous, owns
A shade of sadness in its plaintive tones,
Yet when its breath some loftier thought inspires
Glows with a heat that every bosom fires.
Such Everett seems; no chance-sown wild flower knows
The full-blown charms of culture's double rose,—
Alas, how soon, by death's unsparing frost,
Its bloom is faded and its fragrance lost!

Two voices, only two, to earth belong,
Of all whose accents met the listening throng:
Winthrop, alike for speech and guidance framed,
On that proud day a twofold duty claimed;
One other yet,—remembered or forgot,—
Forgive my silence if I name him not.
Can I believe it? I, whose youthful voice
Claimed a brief gamut,—notes not over choice,
Stood undismayed before the solemn throng,
And *propria voce* sung that saucy song

Which even in memory turns my soul aghast, —
Felix audacia was the verdict cast.

What were the glory of these festal days
Shorn of their grand illumination's blaze?
Night comes at last with all her starry train
To find a light in every glittering pane.
From "Harvard's" windows see the sudden flash, —
Old "Massachusetts" glares through every sash;
From wall to wall the kindling splendors run
Till all is glorious as the noonday sun.

How to the scholar's mind each object brings
What some historian tells, some poet sings!
The good gray teacher whom we all revered —
Loved, honored, laughed at, and by freshmen feared,
As from old "Harvard," where its light began,
From hall to hall the clustering splendors ran —
Took down his well-worn Eschylus and read,
Lit by the rays a thousand tapers shed,
How the swift herald crossed the leagues between
Mycenae's monarch and his faithless queen;
And thus he read, — my verse but ill displays
The Attic picture, clad in modern phrase.

On Ida's summit flames the kindling pile,
And Lemnos answers from his rocky isle;
From Athos next it climbs the reddening skies,
Thence where the watch-towers of Macistus rise.
The sentries of Mesapius in their turn
Bid the dry heath in high piled masses burn,
Cithoeron's crag the crimson billows stain,
Far AEgiplanctus joins the fiery train.
Thus the swift courier through the pathless night
Has gained at length the Arachnoean height,
Whence the glad tidings, borne on wings offlame,
"Ilium has fallen!" reach the royal dame.

So ends the day; before the midnight stroke
The lights expiring cloud the air with smoke;
While these the toil of younger hands employ,
The slumbering Grecian dreams of smouldering Troy.

As to that hour with backward steps I turn,
Midway I pause; behold a funeral urn!

Ah, sad memorial! known but all too well
The tale which thus its golden letters tell:

    This dust, once breathing, changed its joyous life
For toil and hunger, wounds and mortal strife;
Love, friendship, learning's all prevailing charms,
For the cold bivouac and the clash of arms.
The cause of freedom won, a race enslaved
Called back to manhood, and a nation saved,
These sons of Harvard, falling ere their prime,
Leave their proud memory to the coming time.

    While in their still retreats our scholars turn
The mildewed pages of the past, to learn
With endless labor of the sleepless brain
What once has been and ne'er shall be again,
We reap the harvest of their ceaseless toil
And find a fragrance in their midnight oil.
But let a purblind mortal dare the task
The embryo future of itself to ask,
The world reminds him, with a scornful laugh,
That times have changed since Prospero broke his staff.
Could all the wisdom of the schools foretell
The dismal hour when Lisbon shook and fell,
Or name the shuddering night that toppled down
Our sister's pride, beneath whose mural crown
Scarce had the scowl forgot its angry lines,
When earth's blind prisoners fired their fatal mines?

    New realms, new worlds, exulting Science claims,
Still the dim future unexplored remains;
Her trembling scales the far-off planet weigh,
Her torturing prisms its elements betray, —
We know what ores the fires of Sirius melt,
What vaporous metals gild Orion's belt;
Angels, archangels, may have yet to learn
Those hidden truths our heaven-taught eyes discern;
Yet vain is Knowledge, with her mystic wand,
To pierce the cloudy screen and read beyond;
Once to the silent stars the fates were known,
To us they tell no secrets but their own.

    At Israel's altar still we humbly bow,
But where, oh where, are Israel's prophets now?

Where is the sibyl with her hoarded leaves?
Where is the charm the weird enchantress weaves?
No croaking raven turns the auspex pale,
No reeking altars tell the morrow's tale;
The measured footsteps of the Fates are dumb,
Unseen, unheard, unheralded, they come,
Prophet and priest and all their following fail.
Who then is left to rend the future's veil?
Who but the poet, he whose nicer sense
No film can baffle with its slight defence,
Whose finer vision marks the waves that stray,
Felt, but unseen, beyond the violet ray? —
Who, while the storm-wind waits its darkening shroud,
Foretells the tempest ere he sees the cloud, —
Stays not for time his secrets to reveal,
But reads his message ere he breaks the seal.
So Mantua's bard foretold the coming day
Ere Bethlehem's infant in the manger lay;
The promise trusted to a mortal tongue
Found listening ears before the angels sung.
So while his load the creeping pack-horse galled,
While inch by inch the dull canal-boat crawled,
Darwin beheld a Titan from "afar
Drag the slow barge or drive the rapid car,"
That panting giant fed by air and flame,
The mightiest forges task their strength to tame.

Happy the poet! him no tyrant fact
Holds in its clutches to be chained and racked;
Him shall no mouldy document convict,
No stern statistics gravely contradict;
No rival sceptre threats his airy throne;
He rules o'er shadows, but he reigns alone.
Shall I the poet's broad dominion claim
Because you bid me wear his sacred name
For these few moments? Shall I boldly clash
My flint and steel, and by the sudden flash
Read the fair vision which my soul descries
Through the wide pupils of its wondering eyes?
List then awhile; the fifty years have sped;
The third full century's opened scroll is spread,

Blank to all eyes save his who dimly sees
The shadowy future told in words like these.

How strange the prospect to my sight appears,
Changed by the busy hands of fifty years!
Full well I know our ocean-salted Charles,
Filling and emptying through the sands and marls
That wall his restless stream on either bank,
Not all unlovely when the sedges rank
Lend their coarse veil the sable ooze to hide
That bares its blackness with the ebbing tide.
In other shapes to my illumined eyes
Those ragged margins of our stream arise
Through walls of stone the sparkling waters flow,
In clearer depths the golden sunsets glow,
On purer waves the lamps of midnight gleam,
That silver o'er the unpolluted stream.
Along his shores what stately temples rise,
What spires, what turrets, print the shadowed skies!
Our smiling Mother sees her broad domain
Spread its tall roofs along the western plain;
Those blazoned windows' blushing glories tell
Of grateful hearts that loved her long and well;
Yon gilded dome that glitters in the sun
Was Dives' gift,—alas, his only one!
These buttressed walls enshrine a banker's name,
That hallowed chapel hides a miser's shame;
Their wealth they left,—their memory cannot fade
Though age shall crumble every stone they laid.

Great lord of millions,—let me call thee great,
Since countless servants at thy bidding wait,—
Richesse oblige: no mortal must be blind
To all but self, or look at human kind
Laboring and suffering,—all its want and woe,—
Through sheets of crystal, as a pleasing show
That makes life happier for the chosen few
Duty for whom is something not to do.
When thy last page of life at length is filled,
What shall thine heirs to keep thy memory build?
Will piles of stone in Auburn's mournful shade
Save from neglect the spot where thou art laid?
Nay, deem not thus; the sauntering stranger's eye

Will pass unmoved thy columned tombstone by,
No memory wakened, not a teardrop shed,
Thy name uncared for and thy date unread.
But if thy record thou indeed dost prize,
Bid from the soil some stately temple rise,—
Some hall of learning, some memorial shrine,
With names long honored to associate thine:
So shall thy fame outlive thy shattered bust
When all around thee slumber in the dust.
Thus England's Henry lives in Eton's towers,
Saved from the spoil oblivion's gulf devours;
Our later records with as fair a fame
Have wreathed each uncrowned benefactor's name;
The walls they reared the memories still retain
That churchyard marbles try to keep in vain.
In vain the delving antiquary tries
To find the tomb where generous Harvard lies
Here, here, his lasting monument is found,
Where every spot is consecrated ground!
O'er Stoughton's dust the crumbling stone decays,
Fast fade its lines of lapidary praise;
There the wild bramble weaves its ragged nets,
There the dry lichen spreads its gray rosettes;
Still in yon walls his memory lives unspent,
Nor asks a braver, nobler monument.
Thus Hollis lives, and Holden, honored, praised,
And good Sir Matthew, in the halls they raised;
Thus live the worthies of these later times,
Who shine in deeds, less brilliant, grouped in rhymes.
Say, shall the Muse with faltering steps retreat,
Or dare these names in rhythmic form repeat?
Why not as boldly as from Homer's lips
The long array, of Argive battle-ships?
When o'er our graves a thousand years have past
(If to such date our threatened globe shall last)
These classic precincts, myriad feet have pressed,
Will show on high, in beauteous garlands dressed,
Those honored names that grace our later day,—
Weld, Matthews, Sever, Thayer, Austin, Gray,
Sears, Phillips, Lawrence, Hemenway,—to the list
Add Sanders, Sibley,—all the Muse has missed.

Once more I turn to read the pictured page
Bright with the promise of the coming age.
Ye unborn sons of children yet unborn,
Whose youthful eyes shall greet that far-off morn,
Blest are those eyes that all undimmed behold
The sights so longed for by the wise of old.
From high-arched alcoves, through resounding halls,
Clad in full robes majestic Science calls,
Tireless, unsleeping, still at Nature's feet,
Whate'er she utters fearless to repeat,
Her lips at last from every cramp released
That Israel's prophet caught from Egypt's priest.
I see the statesman, firm, sagacious, bold,
For life's long conflict cast in amplest mould;
Not his to clamor with the senseless throng
That shouts unshamed, "Our party, right or wrong,"
But in the patriot's never-ending fight
To side with Truth, who changes wrong to right.
I see the scholar; in that wondrous time
Men, women, children, all can write in rhyme.
These four brief lines addressed to youth inclined
To idle rhyming in his notes I find:

Who writes in verse that should have writ in prose
Is like a traveller walking on his toes;
Happy the rhymester who in time has found
The heels he lifts were made to touch the ground.

I see gray teachers, — on their work intent,
Their lavished lives, in endless labor spent,
Had closed at last in age and penury wrecked,
Martyrs, not burned, but frozen in neglect,
Save for the generous hands that stretched in aid
Of worn-out servants left to die half paid.
Ah, many a year will pass, I thought, ere we
Such kindly forethought shall rejoice to see, —
Monarchs are mindful of the sacred debt
That cold republics hasten to forget.
I see the priest, — if such a name he bears
Who without pride his sacred vestment wears;

And while the symbols of his tribe I seek
Thus my first impulse bids me think and speak:

Let not the mitre England's prelate wears
Next to the crown whose regal pomp it shares,
Though low before it courtly Christians bow,
Leave its red mark on Younger England's brow.
We love, we honor, the maternal dame,
But let her priesthood wear a modest name,
While through the waters of the Pilgrim's bay
A new-born Mayflower shows her keels the way.
Too old grew Britain for her mother's beads, —
Must we be necklaced with her children's creeds?
Welcome alike in surplice or in gown
The loyal lieges of the Heavenly Crown!
We greet with cheerful, not submissive, mien
A sister church, but not a mitred Queen!

A few brief flutters, and the unwilling Muse,
Who feared the flight she hated to refuse,
Shall fold the wings whose gayer plumes are shed,
Here where at first her half-fledged pinions spread.
Well I remember in the long ago
How in the forest shades of Fontainebleau,
Strained through a fissure in a rocky cell,
One crystal drop with measured cadence fell.
Still, as of old, forever bright and clear,
The fissured cavern drops its wonted tear,
And wondrous virtue, simple folk aver,
Lies in that teardrop of la roche qui pleure.

Of old I wandered by the river's side
Between whose banks the mighty waters glide,
Where vast Niagara, hurrying to its fall,
Builds and unbuilds its ever-tumbling wall;
Oft in my dreams I hear the rush and roar
Of battling floods, and feel the trembling shore,
As the huge torrent, girded for its leap,
With bellowing thunders plunges down the steep.
Not less distinct, from memory's pictured urn,

The gray old rock, the leafy woods, return;
Robed in their pride the lofty oaks appear,
And once again with quickened sense I hear,
Through the low murmur of the leaves that stir,
The tinkling teardrop of *la roche qui pleure* .

So when the third ripe century stands complete,
As once again the sons of Harvard meet,
Rejoicing, numerous as the seashore sands,
Drawn from all quarters,—farthest distant lands,
Where through the reeds the scaly saurian steals,
Where cold Alaska feeds her floundering seals,
Where Plymouth, glorying, wears her iron crown,
Where Sacramento sees the suns go down;
Nay, from the cloisters whence the refluent tide
Wafts their pale students to our Mother's side,—
Mid all the tumult that the day shall bring,
While all the echoes shout, and roar, and ring,
These tinkling lines, oblivion's easy prey,
Once more emerging to the light of day,
Not all unpleasing to the listening ear
Shall wake the memories of this bygone year,
Heard as I hear the measured drops that flow
From the gray rock of wooded Fontainebleau.

Yet, ere I leave, one loving word for all
Those fresh young lives that wait our Mother's call:
One gift is yours, kind Nature's richest dower,—
Youth, the fair bud that holds life's opening flower,
Full of high hopes no coward doubts enchain,
With all the future throbbing in its brain,
And mightiest instincts which the beating heart
Fills with the fire its burning waves impart.

O joyous youth, whose glory is to dare,—
Thy foot firm planted on the lowest stair,
Thine eye uplifted to the loftiest height
Where Fame stands beckoning in the rosy light,
Thanks for thy flattering tales, thy fond deceits,
Thy loving lies, thy cheerful smiling cheats
Nature's rash promise every day is broke,—

A thousand acorns breed a single oak,
The myriad blooms that make the orchard gay
In barren beauty throw their lives away;
Yet shall we quarrel with the sap that yields
The painted blossoms which adorn the fields,
When the fair orchard wears its May-day suit
Of pink-white petals, for its scanty fruit?
Thrice happy hours, in hope's illusion dressed,
In fancy's cradle nurtured and caressed,
Though rich the spoils that ripening years may bring,
To thee the dewdrops of the Orient cling, —
Not all the dye-stuffs from the vats of truth
Can match the rainbow on the robes of youth!

    Dear unborn children, to our Mother's trust
We leave you, fearless, when we lie in dust:
While o'er these walls the Christian banner waves
From hallowed lips shall flow the truth that saves;
While o'er those portals Veritas you read
No church shall bind you with its human creed.
Take from the past the best its toil has won,
But learn betimes its slavish ruts to shun.
Pass the old tree whose withered leaves are shed,
Quit the old paths that error loved to tread,
And a new wreath of living blossoms seek,
A narrower pathway up a loftier peak;
Lose not your reverence, but unmanly fear
Leave far behind you, all who enter here!

    As once of old from Ida's lofty height
The flaming signal flashed across the night,
So Harvard's beacon sheds its unspent rays
Till every watch-tower shows its kindling blaze.
Caught from a spark and fanned by every gale,
A brighter radiance gilds the roofs of Yale;
Amherst and Williams bid their flambeaus shine,
And Bowdoin answers through her groves of pine;
O'er Princeton's sands the far reflections steal,
Where mighty Edwards stamped his iron heel;
Nay, on the hill where old beliefs were bound
Fast as if Styx had girt them nine times round,

Bursts such a light that trembling souls inquire
If the whole church of Calvin is on fire!
Well may they ask, for what so brightly burns
As a dry creed that nothing ever learns?
Thus link by link is knit the flaming chain
Lit by the torch of Harvard's hallowed plain.

   Thy son, thy servant, dearest Mother mine,
Lays this poor offering on thy holy shrine,
An autumn leaflet to the wild winds tost,
Touched by the finger of November's frost,
With sweet, sad memories of that earlier day,
And all that listened to my first-born lay.
With grateful heart this glorious morn I see, —
Would that my tribute worthier were of thee!

POST-PRANDIAL

PHI BETA KAPPA

WENDELL PHILLIPS, ORATOR; CHARLES GODFREY LELAND, POET

1881

"THE Dutch have taken Holland," — so the schoolboys used to say;
The Dutch have taken Harvard, — no doubt of that to-day!
For the Wendells were low Dutchmen, and all their vrows were Vans;
And the Breitmanns are high Dutchmen, and here is honest Hans.

Mynheers, you both are welcome! Fair cousin Wendell P.,
Our ancestors were dwellers beside the Zuyder Zee;
Both Grotius and Erasmus were countrymen of we,
And Vondel was our namesake, though he spelt it with a V.

It is well old Evert Jansen sought a dwelling over sea
On the margin of the Hudson, where he sampled you and me
Through our grandsires and great-grandsires, for you would n't quite agree
With the steady-going burghers along the Zuyder Zee.

Like our Motley's John of Barnveld, you have always been inclined
To speak, — well, — somewhat frankly, — to let us know your mind,
And the Mynheers would have told you to be cautious what you said,
Or else that silver tongue of yours might cost your precious head.

But we're very glad you've kept it; it was always Freedom's own,
And whenever Reason chose it she found a royal throne;
You have whacked us with your sceptre; our backs were little harmed,
And while we rubbed our bruises we owned we had been charmed.

And you, our quasi Dutchman, what welcome should be yours
For all the wise prescriptions that work your laughter-cures?
"Shake before taking"?—not a bit,—the bottle-cure's a sham;
Take before shaking, and you 'll find it shakes your diaphragm.

"Hans Breitmann gif a barty,—vhere is dot barty now?"
On every shelf where wit is stored to smooth the careworn brow
A health to stout Hans Breitmann! How long before we see
Another Hans as handsome,—as bright a man as he!

THE FLANEUR

BOSTON COMMON, DECEMBER 6, 1882
DURING THE TRANSIT OF VENUS

I LOVE all sights of earth and skies,
From flowers that glow to stars that shine;
The comet and the penny show,
All curious things, above, below,
Hold each in turn my wandering eyes:
I claim the Christian Pagan's line,
Humani nihil ,—even so,—
And is not human life divine?
When soft the western breezes blow,
And strolling youths meet sauntering maids,
I love to watch the stirring trades
Beneath the Vallombrosa shades
Our much-enduring elms bestow;
The vender and his rhetoric's flow,
That lambent stream of liquid lies;
The bait he dangles from his line,
The gudgeon and his gold-washed prize.
I halt before the blazoned sign
That bids me linger to admire
The drama time can never tire,
The little hero of the hunch,
With iron arm and soul of fire,
And will that works his fierce desire,—
Untamed, unscared, unconquered Punch
My ear a pleasing torture finds
In tones the withered sibyl grinds,—
The dame sans merci's broken strain,
Whom I erewhile, perchance, have known,
When Orleans filled the Bourbon throne,
A siren singing by the Seine.

But most I love the tube that spies
The orbs celestial in their march;
That shows the comet as it whisks
Its tail across the planets' disks,
As if to blind their blood-shot eyes;
Or wheels so close against the sun
We tremble at the thought of risks
Our little spinning ball may run,
To pop like corn that children parch,
From summer something overdone,
And roll, a cinder, through the skies.

Grudge not to-day the scanty fee
To him who farms the firmament,
To whom the Milky Way is free;
Who holds the wondrous crystal key,
The silent Open Sesame
That Science to her sons has lent;
Who takes his toll, and lifts the bar
That shuts the road to sun and star.
If Venus only comes to time,
(And prophets say she must and shall,)
To-day will hear the tinkling chime
Of many a ringing silver dime,
For him whose optic glass supplies
The crowd with astronomic eyes,—
The Galileo of the Mall.

Dimly the transit morning broke;
The sun seemed doubting what to do,
As one who questions how to dress,
And takes his doublets from the press,
And halts between the old and new.
Please Heaven he wear his suit of blue,
Or don, at least, his ragged cloak,
With rents that show the azure through!

I go the patient crowd to join
That round the tube my eyes discern,
The last new-comer of the file,
And wait, and wait, a weary while,

And gape, and stretch, and shrug, and smile,
(For each his place must fairly earn,

Hindmost and foremost, in his turn,)
Till hitching onward, pace by pace,
I gain at last the envied place,
And pay the white exiguous coin:
The sun and I are face to face;
He glares at me, I stare at him;
And lo! my straining eye has found
A little spot that, black and round,
Lies near the crimsoned fire-orb's rim.
O blessed, beauteous evening star,
Well named for her whom earth adores,—
The Lady of the dove-drawn car,—
I know thee in thy white simar;
But veiled in black, a rayless spot,
Blank as a careless scribbler's blot,
Stripped of thy robe of silvery flame,—
The stolen robe that Night restores
When Day has shut his golden doors,—
I see thee, yet I know thee not;
And canst thou call thyself the same?

A black, round spot,—and that is all;
And such a speck our earth would be
If he who looks upon the stars
Through the red atmosphere of Mars
Could see our little creeping ball
Across the disk of crimson crawl
As I our sister planet see.

And art thou, then, a world like ours,
Flung from the orb that whirled our own
A molten pebble from its zone?
How must thy burning sands absorb
The fire-waves of the blazing orb,
Thy chain so short, thy path so near,
Thy flame-defying creatures hear
The maelstroms of the photosphere!
And is thy bosom decked with flowers
That steal their bloom from scalding showers?
And hast thou cities, domes, and towers,
And life, and love that makes it dear,
And death that fills thy tribes with fear?

Lost in my dream, my spirit soars
Through paths the wandering angels know;
My all-pervading thought explores
The azure ocean's lucent shores;
I leave my mortal self below,
As up the star-lit stairs I climb,
And still the widening view reveals
In endless rounds the circling wheels
That build the horologe of time.
New spheres, new suns, new systems gleam;
The voice no earth-born echo hears
Steals softly on my ravished ears
I hear them "singing as they shine" —
A mortal's voice dissolves my dream:
My patient neighbor, next in line,
Hints gently there are those who wait.
O guardian of the starry gate,
What coin shall pay this debt of mine?
Too slight thy claim, too small the fee
That bids thee turn the potent key.

The Tuscan's hand has placed in thine.
Forgive my own the small affront,
The insult of the proffered dime;
Take it, O friend, since this thy wont,
But still shall faithful memory be
A bankrupt debtor unto thee,
And pay thee with a grateful rhyme.

AVE

PRELUDE TO "ILLUSTRATED POEMS"

FULL well I know the frozen hand has come
That smites the songs of grove and garden dumb,
And chills sad autumn's last chrysanthemum;

Yet would I find one blossom, if I might,
Ere the dark loom that weaves the robe of white
Hides all the wrecks of summer out of sight.

Sometimes in dim November's narrowing day,
When all the season's pride has passed away,
As mid the blackened stems and leaves we stray,

We spy in sheltered nook or rocky cleft
A starry disk the hurrying winds have left,
Of all its blooming sisterhood bereft.

Some pansy, with its wondering baby eyes
Poor wayside nursling!—fixed in blank surprise
At the rough welcome of unfriendly skies;

Or golden daisy,—will it dare disclaim
The lion's tooth, to wear this gentler name?
Or blood-red salvia, with its lips aflame.

The storms have stripped the lily and the rose,
Still on its cheek the flush of summer glows,
And all its heart-leaves kindle as it blows.

So had I looked some bud of song to find
The careless winds of autumn left behind,
With these of earlier seasons' growth to bind.

Ah me! my skies are dark with sudden grief,
A flower lies faded on my garnered sheaf;
Yet let the sunshine gild this virgin leaf,

The joyous, blessed sunshine of the past,
Still with me, though the heavens are overcast, —
The light that shines while life and memory last.

Go, pictured rhymes, for loving readers meant;
Bring back the smiles your jocund morning lent,
And warm their hearts with sunbeams yet unspent!

BEVERLY FARMS, July 24, 1884.

KING'S CHAPEL

READ AT THE TWO HUNDREDTH ANNIVERSARY

Is it a weanling's weakness for the past
That in the stormy, rebel-breeding town,
Swept clean of relics by the levelling blast,

Still keeps our gray old chapel's name of "King's,"
Still to its outworn symbols fondly clings, —
Its unchurched mitres and its empty crown?

Poor harmless emblems! All has shrunk away
That made them gorgons in the patriot's eyes;
The priestly plaything harms us not to-day;
The gilded crown is but a pleasing show,
An old-world heirloom, left from long ago,
Wreck of the past that memory bids us prize,

Lightly we glance the fresh-cut marbles o'er;
Those two of earlier date our eyes enthrall:
The proud old Briton's by the western door,
And hers, the Lady of Colonial days,
Whose virtues live in long-drawn classic phrase, —
The fair Francesca of the southern wall.

Ay! those were goodly men that Reynolds drew,
And stately dames our Copley's canvas holds,
To their old Church, their Royal Master, true,
Proud of the claim their valiant sires had earned,
That "gentle blood," not lightly to be spurned,
Save by the churl ungenerous Nature moulds.

All vanished! It were idle to complain
That ere the fruits shall come the flowers must fall;
Yet somewhat we have lost amidst our gain,
Some rare ideals time may not restore, —
The charm of courtly breeding, seen no more,
And reverence, dearest ornament of all.

Thus musing, to the western wall I came,
Departing: lo! a tablet fresh and fair,
Where glistened many a youth's remembered name
In golden letters on the snow-white stone, —
Young lives these aisles and arches once have known,
Their country's bleeding altar might not spare.

These died that we might claim a soil unstained,
Save by the blood of heroes; their bequests
A realm unsevered and a race unchained.
Has purer blood through Norman veins come down
From the rough knights that clutched the Saxon's crown
Than warmed the pulses in these faithful breasts?

These, too, shall live in history's deathless page,
High on the slow-wrought pedestals of fame,
Ranged with the heroes of remoter age;
They could not die who left their nation free,
Firm as the rock, unfettered as the sea,
Its heaven unshadowed by the cloud of shame.

While on the storied past our memory dwells,
Our grateful tribute shall not be denied, —
The wreath, the cross of rustling immortelles;
And willing hands shall clear each darkening bust,
As year by year sifts down the clinging dust
On Shirley's beauty and on Vassall's pride.

But for our own, our loved and lost, we bring
With throbbing hearts and tears that still must flow,
In full-heaped hands, the opening flowers of spring,
Lilies half-blown, and budding roses, red
As their young cheeks, before the blood was shed
That lent their morning bloom its generous glow.

Ah, who shall count a rescued nation's debt,
Or sum in words our martyrs' silent claims?
Who shall our heroes' dread exchange forget, —
All life, youth, hope, could promise to allure
For all that soul could brave or flesh endure?
They shaped our future; we but carve their names.

HYMN

SUNG BY THE CONGREGATION TO THE TUNE OF TALLIS'S EVENING HYMN

O'ERSHADOWED by the walls that climb,
Piled up in air by living hands,
A rock amid the waves of time,
Our gray old house of worship stands.

High o'er the pillared aisles we love
The symbols of the past look down;
Unharmed, unharming, throned above,
Behold the mitre and the crown!

Let not our younger faith forget
The loyal souls that held them dear;
The prayers we read their tears have wet,
The hymns we sing they loved to hear.

The memory of their earthly throne
Still to our holy temple clings,
But here the kneeling suppliants own
One only Lord, the King of kings.

Hark! while our hymn of grateful praise
The solemn echoing vaults prolong,
The far-off voice of earlier days
Blends with our own in hallowed song:

To Him who ever lives and reigns,
Whom all the hosts of heaven adore,
Who lent the life His breath sustains,
Be glory now and evermore!

HYMN.—THE WORD OF PROMISE

(by supposition)

An Hymn set forth to be sung by the Great
Assembly at Newtown, [Mass.] Mo. 12. 1. 1636.

[Written by OLIVER WENDELL HOLMES, eldest son of Rev.
ABIEL HOLMES, eighth Pastor of the First Church in
Cambridge, Massachusetts.]

LORD, Thou hast led us as of old
Thine Arm led forth the chosen Race
Through Foes that raged, through Floods that roll'd,
To Canaan's far-off Dwelling-Place.

Here is Thy bounteous Table spread,
Thy Manna falls on every Field,
Thy Grace our hungering Souls hath fed,
Thy Might hath been our Spear and Shield.

Lift high Thy Buckler, Lord of Hosts!
Guard Thou Thy Servants, Sons and Sires,
While on the Godless heathen Coasts
They light Thine Israel's Altar-fires!

The salvage Wilderness remote
Shall hear Thy Works and Wonders sung;
So from the Rock that Moses smote
The Fountain of the Desart sprung.

Soon shall the slumbering Morn awake,
From wandering Stars of Errour freed,
When Christ the Bread of Heaven shall break
For Saints that own a common Creed.

The Walls that fence His Flocks apart
Shall crack and crumble in Decay,
And every Tongue and every Heart
Shall welcome in the new-born Day.

Then shall His glorious Church rejoice
His Word of Promise to recall, —
ONE SHELTERING FOLD, ONE SHEPHERD'S VOICE,
ONE GOD AND FATHER OVER ALL!

HYMN

READ AT THE DEDICATION OF THE OLIVER WENDELL
HOLMES HOSPITAL AT HUDSON, WISCONSIN
JUNE 7, 1877

ANGEL of love, for every grief
Its soothing balm thy mercy brings,
For every pang its healing leaf,
For homeless want, thine outspread, wings.

Enough for thee the pleading eye,
The knitted brow of silent pain;
The portals open to a sigh
Without the clank of bolt or chain.

Who is our brother? He that lies
Left at the wayside, bruised and sore
His need our open hand supplies,
His welcome waits him at our door.

Not ours to ask in freezing tones
His race, his calling, or his creed;
Each heart the tie of kinship owns,
When those are human veins that bleed.

Here stand the champions to defend
From every wound that flesh can feel;
Here science, patience, skill, shall blend
To save, to calm, to help, to heal.

Father of Mercies! Weak and frail,
Thy guiding hand Thy children ask;
Let not the Great Physician fail
To aid us in our holy task.

Source of all truth, and love, and light,
That warm and cheer our earthly days,
Be ours to serve Thy will aright,
Be Thine the glory and the praise!

ON THE DEATH OF PRESIDENT GARFIELD

I.

FALLEN with autumn's falling leaf
Ere yet his summer's noon was past,
Our friend, our guide, our trusted chief,—
What words can match a woe so vast!

And whose the chartered claim to speak
The sacred grief where all have part,
Where sorrow saddens every cheek
And broods in every aching heart?

Yet Nature prompts the burning phrase
That thrills the hushed and shrouded hall,
The loud lament, the sorrowing praise,
The silent tear that love lets fall.

In loftiest verse, in lowliest rhyme,
Shall strive unblamed the minstrel choir,—-
The singers of the new-born time,
And trembling age with outworn lyre.

No room for pride, no place for blame,—
We fling our blossoms on the grave,
Pale,—scentless,—faded,—all we claim,
This only,—what we had we gave.

Ah, could the grief of all who mourn
Blend in one voice its bitter cry,
The wail to heaven's high arches borne
Would echo through the caverned sky.

II.

O happiest land, whose peaceful choice
Fills with a breath its empty throne!
God, speaking through thy people's voice,
Has made that voice for once His own.

No angry passion shakes the state
Whose weary servant seeks for rest;

And who could fear that scowling hate
Would strike at that unguarded breast?

He stands, unconscious of his doom,
In manly strength, erect, serene;
Around him Summer spreads her bloom;
He falls,—what horror clothes the scene!

How swift the sudden flash of woe
Where all was bright as childhood's dream!
As if from heaven's ethereal bow
Had leaped the lightning's arrowy gleam.

Blot the foul deed from history's page;
Let not the all-betraying sun
Blush for the day that stains an age
When murder's blackest wreath was won.

III.

Pale on his couch the sufferer lies,
The weary battle-ground of pain
Love tends his pillow; Science tries
Her every art, alas! in vain.

The strife endures how long! how long!
Life, death, seem balanced in the scale,
While round his bed a viewless throng
Await each morrow's changing tale.

In realms the desert ocean parts
What myriads watch with tear-filled eyes,
His pulse-beats echoing in their hearts,
His breathings counted with their sighs!

Slowly the stores of life are spent,
Yet hope still battles with despair;
Will Heaven not yield when knees are bent?
Answer, O thou that hearest prayer.

But silent is the brazen sky;
On sweeps the meteor's threatening train,
Unswerving Nature's mute reply,
Bound in her adamantine chain.

Not ours the verdict to decide
Whom death shall claim or skill shall save;

The hero's life though Heaven denied,
It gave our land a martyr's grave.

Nor count the teaching vainly sent
How human hearts their griefs may share,—
The lesson woman's love has lent,
What hope may do, what faith can bear!

Farewell! the leaf-strown earth enfolds
Our stay, our pride, our hopes, our fears,
And autumn's golden sun beholds
A nation bowed, a world in tears.

THE GOLDEN FLOWER

WHEN Advent dawns with lessening days,
While earth awaits the angels' hymn;
When bare as branching coral sways
In whistling winds each leafless limb;
When spring is but a spendthrift's dream,
And summer's wealth a wasted dower,
Nor dews nor sunshine may redeem, —
Then autumn coins his Golden Flower.

Soft was the violet's vernal hue,
Fresh was the rose's morning red,
Full-orbed the stately dahlia grew, —
All gone! their short-lived splendors shed.
The shadows, lengthening, stretch at noon;
The fields are stripped, the groves are dumb;
The frost-flowers greet the icy moon, —
Then blooms the bright chrysanthemum.

The stiffening turf is white with snow,
Yet still its radiant disks are seen
Where soon the hallowed morn will show
The wreath and cross of Christmas green;
As if in autumn's dying days
It heard the heavenly song afar,
And opened all its glowing rays,
The herald lamp of Bethlehem's star.

Orphan of summer, kindly sent
To cheer the fading year's decline,
In all that pitying Heaven has lent
No fairer pledge of hope than thine.
Yes! June lies hid beneath the snow,

And winter's unborn heir shall claim
For every seed that sleeps below
A spark that kindles into flame.

    Thy smile the scowl of winter braves
Last of the bright-robed, flowery train,
Soft sighing o'er the garden graves,
"Farewell! farewell! we meet again!"
So may life's chill November bring
Hope's golden flower, the last of all,
Before we hear the angels sing
Where blossoms never fade and fall!

HAIL, COLUMBIA!

1798

THE FIRST VERSE OF THE SONG
BY JOSEPH HOPKINSON

"HAIL, Columbia! Happy land!
Hail, ye heroes, heaven-born band,
Who fought and bled in Freedom's cause,
Who fought and bled in Freedom's cause,
And when the storm of war was gone
Enjoy'd the peace your valor won.
Let independence be our boast,
Ever mindful what it cost;
Ever grateful for the prize,
Let its altar reach the skies.

"Firm—united—let us be,
Rallying round our Liberty;
As a band of brothers join'd,
Peace and safety we shall find."

ADDITIONAL VERSES

WRITTEN AT THE REQUEST OF THE COMMITTEE FOR THE CONSTITUTIONAL CENTENNIAL CELEBRATION AT PHILADELPHIA,

1887

LOOK our ransomed shores around,
Peace and safety we have found!
Welcome, friends who once were foes!
Welcome, friends who once were foes,
To all the conquering years have gained, —
A nation's rights, a race unchained!

Children of the day new-born,
Mindful of its glorious morn,
Let the pledge our fathers signed
Heart to heart forever bind!

While the stars of heaven shall burn,
While the ocean tides return,
Ever may the circling sun
Find the Many still are One!

Graven deep with edge of steel,
Crowned with Victory's crimson seal,
All the world their names shall read!
All the world their names shall read,
Enrolled with his, the Chief that led
The hosts whose blood for us was shed.
Pay our sires their children's debt,
Love and honor, nor forget
Only Union's golden key
Guards the Ark of Liberty!

While the stars of heaven shall burn,
While the ocean tides return,
Ever may the circling sun
Find the Many still are One!

Hail, Columbia! strong and free,
Throned in hearts from sea to sea
Thy march triumphant still pursue!
Thy march triumphant still pursue
With peaceful stride from zone to zone,
Till Freedom finds the world her own.

Blest in Union's holy ties,
Let our grateful song arise,
Every voice its tribute lend,
All in loving chorus blend!

While the stars in heaven shall burn,
While the ocean tides return,
Ever shall the circling sun
Find the Many still are One!

POEM

FOR THE DEDICATION OF THE FOUNTAIN AT STRATFORD-ON-AVON, PRESENTED BY GEORGE W. CHILDS, OF PHILADELPHIA

WELCOME, thrice welcome is thy silvery gleam,
Thou long-imprisoned stream!
Welcome the tinkle of thy crystal beads
As plashing raindrops to the flowery meads,
As summer's breath to Avon's whispering reeds!
From rock-walled channels, drowned in rayless night,
Leap forth to life and light;
Wake from the darkness of thy troubled dream,
And greet with answering smile the morning's beam!

No purer lymph the white-limbed Naiad knows
Than from thy chalice flows;
Not the bright spring of Afric's sunny shores,
Starry with spangles washed from golden ores,
Nor glassy stream Bandusia's fountain pours,
Nor wave translucent where Sabrina fair
Braids her loose-flowing hair,
Nor the swift current, stainless as it rose
Where chill Arveiron steals from Alpine snows.

Here shall the traveller stay his weary feet
To seek thy calm retreat;
Here at high noon the brown-armed reaper rest;
Here, when the shadows, lengthening from the west,
Call the mute song-bird to his leafy nest,
Matron and maid shall chat the cares away
That brooded o'er the day,
While flocking round them troops of children meet,
And all the arches ring with laughter sweet.

Here shall the steed, his patient life who spends
In toil that never ends,

Hot from his thirsty tramp o'er hill and plain,
Plunge his red nostrils, while the torturing rein
Drops in loose loops beside his floating mane;
Nor the poor brute that shares his master's lot
Find his small needs forgot, —
Truest of humble, long-enduring friends,
Whose presence cheers, whose guardian care
defends!

Here lark and thrush and nightingale shall sip,
And skimming swallows dip,
And strange shy wanderers fold their lustrous plumes
Fragrant from bowers that lent their sweet perfumes
Where Paestum's rose or Persia's lilac blooms;
Here from his cloud the eagle stoop to drink
At the full basin's brink,
And whet his beak against its rounded lip,
His glossy feathers glistening as they drip.

Here shall the dreaming poet linger long,
Far from his listening throng, —
Nor lute nor lyre his trembling hand shall bring;
Here no frail Muse shall imp her crippled wing,
No faltering minstrel strain his throat to sing!
These hallowed echoes who shall dare to claim
Whose tuneless voice would shame,
Whose jangling chords with jarring notes would wrong
The nymphs that heard the Swan if Avon's song?

What visions greet the pilgrim's raptured eyes!
What ghosts made real rise!
The dead return, — they breathe, — they live again,
Joined by the host of Fancy's airy train,
Fresh from the springs of Shakespeare's quickening brain!
The stream that slakes the soul's diviner thirst
Here found the sunbeams first;
Rich with his fame, not less shall memory prize
The gracious gift that humbler wants supplies.

O'er the wide waters reached the hand that gave
To all this bounteous wave,
With health and strength and joyous beauty fraught;
Blest be the generous pledge of friendship, brought
From the far home of brothers' love, unbought!

Long may fair Avon's fountain flow, enrolled
With storied shrines of old,
Castalia's spring, Egeria's dewy cave,
And Horeb's rock the God of Israel slave!

Land of our fathers, ocean makes us two,
But heart to heart is true!
Proud is your towering daughter in the West,
Yet in her burning life-blood reign confest
Her mother's pulses beating in her breast.
This holy fount, whose rills from heaven descend,
Its gracious drops shall lend,—
Both foreheads bathed in that baptismal dew,
And love make one the old home and the new!

August 29, 1887.

TO THE POETS WHO ONLY READ AND LISTEN

WHEN evening's shadowy fingers fold
The flowers of every hue,
Some shy, half-opened bud will hold
Its drop of morning's dew.

Sweeter with every sunlit hour
The trembling sphere has grown,
Till all the fragrance of the flower
Becomes at last its own.

We that have sung perchance may find
Our little meed of praise,
And round our pallid temples bind
The wreath of fading bays.

Ah, Poet, who hast never spent
Thy breath in idle strains,
For thee the dewdrop morning lent
Still in thy heart remains;

Unwasted, in its perfumed cell
It waits the evening gale;
Then to the azure whence it fell
Its lingering sweets exhale.

FOR THE DEDICATION OF THE NEW CITY LIBRARY, BOSTON

PROUDLY, beneath her glittering dome,
Our three-hilled city greets the morn;
Here Freedom found her virgin home, —
The Bethlehem where her babe was born.

The lordly roofs of traffic rise
Amid the smoke of household fires;
High o'er them in the peaceful skies
Faith points to heaven her clustering spires.

Can Freedom breathe if ignorance reign?
Shall Commerce thrive where anarchs rule?
Will Faith her half-fledged brood retain
If darkening counsels cloud the school?

Let in the light! from every age
Some gleams of garnered wisdom pour,
And, fixed on thought's electric page,
Wait all their radiance to restore.

Let in the light! in diamond mines
Their gems invite the hand that delves;
So learning's treasured jewels shine
Ranged on the alcove's ordered shelves.

From history's scroll the splendor streams,
From science leaps the living ray;
Flashed from the poet's glowing dreams
The opal fires of fancy play.

Let in the light! these windowed walls
Shall brook no shadowing colonnades,
But day shall flood the silent halls
Till o'er yon hills the sunset fades.

Behind the ever open gate
No pikes shall fence a crumbling throne,

No lackeys cringe, no courtiers wait,
This palace is the people's own!

Heirs of our narrow-girdled past,
How fair the prospect we survey,
Where howled unheard the wintry blast,
And rolled unchecked the storm-swept bay!

These chosen precincts, set apart
For learned toil and holy shrines,
Yield willing homes to every art
That trains, or strengthens, or refines.

Here shall the sceptred mistress reign
Who heeds her meanest subject's call,
Sovereign of all their vast domain,
The queen, the handmaid of them all!

November 26, 1888.

FOR THE WINDOW IN ST. MARGARET'S IN MEMORY OF A SON OF ARCHDEACON FARRAR

AFAR he sleeps whose name is graven here,
Where loving hearts his early doom deplore;
Youth, promise, virtue, all that made him dear
Heaven lent, earth borrowed, sorrowing to restore.

BOSTON, April 12, 1891.

JAMES RUSSELL LOWELL

1819-1891

THOU shouldst have sung the swan-song for the choir
That filled our groves with music till the day
Lit the last hilltop with its reddening fire,
And evening listened for thy lingering lay.

But thou hast found thy voice in realms afar
Where strains celestial blend their notes with thine;
Some cloudless sphere beneath a happier star
Welcomes the bright-winged spirit we resign.

How Nature mourns thee in the still retreat
Where passed in peace thy love-enchanted hours!
Where shall she find an eye like thine to greet
Spring's earliest footprints on her opening flowers?

Have the pale wayside weeds no fond regret
For him who read the secrets they enfold?
Shall the proud spangles of the field forget
The verse that lent new glory to their gold?

And ye whose carols wooed his infant ear,
Whose chants with answering woodnotes he repaid,
Have ye no song his spirit still may hear
From Elmwood's vaults of overarching shade?

Friends of his studious hours, who thronged to teach
The deep-read scholar all your varied lore,
Shall he no longer seek your shelves to reach
The treasure missing from his world-wide store?

This singer whom we long have held so dear
Was Nature's darling, shapely, strong, and fair;
Of keenest wit, of judgment crystal-clear,
Easy of converse, courteous, debonair,

Fit for the loftiest or the lowliest lot,
Self-poised, imperial, yet of simplest ways;

At home alike in castle or in cot,
True to his aim, let others blame or praise.

Freedom he found an heirloom from his sires;
Song, letters, statecraft, shared his years in turn;
All went to feed the nation's altar-fires
Whose mourning children wreathe his funeral urn.

He loved New England,—people, language, soil,
Unweaned by exile from her arid breast.
Farewell awhile, white-handed son of toil,
Go with her brown-armed laborers to thy rest.

Peace to thy slumber in the forest shade!
Poet and patriot, every gift was thine;
Thy name shall live while summers bloom and fade,
And grateful Memory guard thy leafy shrine!

===

POEMS FROM OVER THE TEACUPS

TO THE ELEVEN LADIES

WHO PRESENTED ME WITH A SILVER LOVING CUP ON THE TWENTY-NINTH OF AUGUST, M DCCC LXXXIX

"WHO gave this cup?" The secret thou wouldst steal
Its brimming flood forbids it to reveal:
No mortal's eye shall read it till he first
Cool the red throat of thirst.

If on the golden floor one draught remain,
Trust me, thy careful search will be in vain;
Not till the bowl is emptied shalt thou know
The names enrolled below.

Deeper than Truth lies buried in her well
Those modest names the graven letters spell
Hide from the sight; but wait, and thou shalt see
Who the good angels be.

Whose bounty glistens in the beauteous gift
That friendly hands to loving lips shall lift
Turn the fair goblet when its floor is dry,—
Their names shall meet thine eye.

Count thou their number on the beads of Heaven
Alas! the clustered Pleiads are but seven;
Nay, the nine sister Muses are too few,—
The Graces must add two.

"For whom this gift?" For one who all too long
Clings to his bough among the groves of song;
Autumn's last leaf, that spreads its faded wing
To greet a second spring.

Dear friends, kind friends, whate'er the cup may hold,
Bathing its burnished depths, will change to gold
Its last bright drop let thirsty Maenads drain,
Its fragrance will remain.

Better love's perfume in the empty bowl
Than wine's nepenthe for the aching soul;
Sweeter than song that ever poet sung,
It makes an old heart young!

THE PEAU DE CHAGRIN OF STATE STREET

How beauteous is the bond
In the manifold array
Of its promises to pay,
While the eight per cent it gives
And the rate at which one lives
Correspond!

But at last the bough is bare
Where the coupons one by one
Through their ripening days have run,
And the bond, a beggar now,
Seeks investment anyhow,
Anywhere!

CACOETHES SCRIBENDI

IF all the trees in all the woods were men;
And each and every blade of grass a pen;
If every leaf on every shrub and tree
Turned to a sheet of foolscap; every sea
Were changed to ink, and all earth's living tribes
Had nothing else to do but act as scribes,
And for ten thousand ages, day and night,
The human race should write, and write, and write,
Till all the pens and paper were used up,
And the huge inkstand was an empty cup,
Still would the scribblers clustered round its brink
Call for more pens, more paper, and more ink.

THE ROSE AND THE FERN

LADY, life's sweetest lesson wouldst thou learn,
Come thou with me to Love's enchanted bower
High overhead the trellised roses burn;
Beneath thy feet behold the feathery fern, —
A leaf without a flower.

What though the rose leaves fall? They still are sweet,
And have been lovely in their beauteous prime,
While the bare frond seems ever to repeat,
"For us no bud, no blossom, wakes to greet
The joyous flowering time!"

Heed thou the lesson. Life has leaves to tread
And flowers to cherish; summer round thee glows;
Wait not till autumn's fading robes are shed,
But while its petals still are burning red
Gather life's full-blown rose!

I LIKE YOU AND I LOVE YOU

I LIKE YOU Met I LOVE You, face to face;
The path was narrow, and they could not pass.
I LIKE YOU smiled; I LOVE YOU cried, Alas!
And so they halted for a little space.

"Turn thou and go before," I LOVE YOU said,
"Down the green pathway, bright with many a flower;
Deep in the valley, lo! my bridal bower
Awaits thee." But I LIKE YOU shook his head.

Then while they lingered on the span-wide shelf
That shaped a pathway round the rocky ledge,
I LIKE You bared his icy dagger's edge,
And first he slew I LOVE You,—then himself.

LA MAISON D'OR

(BAR HARBOR)

FROM this fair home behold on either side
The restful mountains or the restless sea
So the warm sheltering walls of life divide
Time and its tides from still eternity.

Look on the waves: their stormy voices teach
That not on earth may toil and struggle cease.
Look on the mountains: better far than speech
Their silent promise of eternal peace.

TOO YOUNG FOR LOVE

Too young for love?
Ah, say not so!
Tell reddening rose-buds not to blow
Wait not for spring to pass away,—
Love's summer months begin with May!
Too young for love?
Ah, say not so!
Too young? Too young?
Ah, no! no! no!

Too young for love?
Ah, say not so,
To practise all love learned in May.
June soon will come with lengthened day
While daisies bloom and tulips glow!

Too young for love?
Ah, say not so!
Too young? Too young?
Ah, no! no! no!

THE BROOMSTICK TRAIN; OR, THE RETURN OF THE WITCHES

LOOK out! Look out, boys! Clear the track!
The witches are here! They've all come back!
They hanged them high,—No use! No use!
What cares a witch for a hangman's noose?
They buried them deep, but they wouldn't lie still,
For cats and witches are hard to kill;
They swore they shouldn't and wouldn't die,—
Books said they did, but they lie! they lie!

A couple of hundred years, or so,
They had knocked about in the world below,
When an Essex Deacon dropped in to call,
And a homesick feeling seized them all;
For he came from a place they knew full well,
And many a tale he had to tell.
They longed to visit the haunts of men,
To see the old dwellings they knew again,
And ride on their broomsticks all around
Their wide domain of unhallowed ground.

In Essex county there's many a roof
Well known to him of the cloven hoof;
The small square windows are full in view
Which the midnight hags went sailing through,
On their well-trained broomsticks mounted high,
Seen like shadows against the sky;
Crossing the track of owls and bats,
Hugging before them their coal-black cats.

Well did they know, those gray old wives,
The sights we see in our daily drives
Shimmer of lake and shine of sea,
Browne's bare hill with its lonely tree,
(It was n't then as we see it now,

With one scant scalp-lock to shade its brow;)
Dusky nooks in the Essex woods,
Dark, dim, Dante-like solitudes,
Where the tree-toad watches the sinuous snake
Glide through his forests of fern and brake;
Ipswich River; its old stone bridge;
Far off Andover's Indian Ridge,
And many a scene where history tells
Some shadow of bygone terror dwells,—
Of "Norman's Woe" with its tale of dread,
Of the Screeching Woman of Marblehead,
(The fearful story that turns men pale
Don't bid me tell it,—my speech would fail.)

Who would not, will not, if he can,
Bathe in the breezes of fair Cape Ann,—
Rest in the bowers her bays enfold,
Loved by the sachems and squaws of old?
Home where the white magnolias bloom,
Sweet with the bayberry's chaste perfume,
Hugged by the woods and kissed by the sea!
Where is the Eden like to thee?
For that "couple of hundred years, or so,"
There had been no peace in the world below;
The witches still grumbling, "It is n't fair;
Come, give us a taste of the upper air!
We 've had enough of your sulphur springs,
And the evil odor that round them clings;
We long for a drink that is cool and nice,—
Great buckets of water with Wenham ice;
We've served you well up-stairs, you know;
You 're a good old—fellow—come, let us go!"

I don't feel sure of his being good,
But he happened to be in a pleasant mood,—
As fiends with their skins full sometimes are,—
(He'd been drinking with "roughs" at a Boston bar.)
So what does he do but up and shout
To a graybeard turnkey, "Let 'em out!"

To mind his orders was all he knew;
The gates swung open, and out they flew.
"Where are our broomsticks?" the beldams cried.
"Here are your broomsticks," an imp replied.

"They 've been in—the place you know—so long
They smell of brimstone uncommon strong;
But they've gained by being left alone,—
Just look, and you'll see how tall they've grown."
"And where is my cat?" a vixen squalled.
"Yes, where are our cats?" the witches bawled,
And began to call them all by name
As fast as they called the cats, they came
There was bob-tailed Tommy and long-tailed Tim,
And wall-eyed Jacky and green-eyed Jim,
And splay-foot Benny and slim-legged Beau,
And Skinny and Squally, and Jerry and Joe,
And many another that came at call,—
It would take too long to count them all.
All black,—one could hardly tell which was which,
But every cat knew his own old witch;
And she knew hers as hers knew her,—
Ah, didn't they curl their tails and purr!

No sooner the withered hags were free
Than out they swarmed for a midnight spree;
I couldn't tell all they did in rhymes,
But the Essex people had dreadful times.
The Swampscott fishermen still relate
How a strange sea-monster stole their bait;
How their nets were tangled in loops and knots,
And they found dead crabs in their lobster-pots.
Poor Danvers grieved for her blasted crops,
And Wilmington mourned over mildewed hops.
A blight played havoc with Beverly beans,—
It was all the work of those hateful queans!
A dreadful panic began at "Pride's,"
Where the witches stopped in their midnight rides,
And there rose strange rumors and vague alarms
'Mid the peaceful dwellers at Beverly Farms.

Now when the Boss of the Beldams found
That without his leave they were ramping round,
He called,—they could hear him twenty miles,
From Chelsea beach to the Misery Isles;
The deafest old granny knew his tone
Without the trick of the telephone.
"Come here, you witches! Come here!" says he,—

"At your games of old, without asking me!
I'll give you a little job to do
That will keep you stirring, you godless crew!"

They came, of course, at their master's call,
The witches, the broomsticks, the cats, and all;
He led the hags to a railway train
The horses were trying to drag in vain.
"Now, then," says he, "you've had your fun,
And here are the cars you've got to run.
The driver may just unhitch his team,
We don't want horses, we don't want steam;
You may keep your old black cats to hug,
But the loaded train you've got to lug."

Since then on many a car you 'll see
A broomstick plain as plain can be;
On every stick there's a witch astride, —
The string you see to her leg is tied.
She will do a mischief if she can,
But the string is held by a careful man,
And whenever the evil-minded witch
Would cut some caper, he gives a twitch.
As for the hag, you can't see her,
But hark! you can hear her black cat's purr,
And now and then, as a car goes by,
You may catch a gleam from her wicked eye.

Often you've looked on a rushing train,
But just what moved it was not so plain.
It couldn't be those wires above,
For they could neither pull nor shove;
Where was the motor that made it go
You couldn't guess, but now you know.

Remember my rhymes when you ride again
On the rattling rail by the broomstick train!

TARTARUS

WHILE in my simple gospel creed
That "God is Love" so plain I read,
Shall dreams of heathen birth affright
My pathway through the coming night?
Ah, Lord of life, though spectres pale
Fill with their threats the shadowy vale,
With Thee my faltering steps to aid,
How can I dare to be afraid?

Shall mouldering page or fading scroll
Outface the charter of the soul?
Shall priesthood's palsied arm protect
The wrong our human hearts reject,
And smite the lips whose shuddering cry
Proclaims a cruel creed a lie?
The wizard's rope we disallow
Was justice once, — is murder now!

Is there a world of blank despair,
And dwells the Omnipresent there?
Does He behold with smile serene
The shows of that unending scene,
Where sleepless, hopeless anguish lies,
And, ever dying, never dies?
Say, does He hear the sufferer's groan,
And is that child of wrath his own?

O mortal, wavering in thy trust,
Lift thy pale forehead from the dust!
The mists that cloud thy darkened eyes
Fade ere they reach the o'erarching skies
When the blind heralds of despair
Would bid thee doubt a Father's care,
Look up from earth, and read above
On heaven's blue tablet, GOD IS LOVE!

AT THE TURN OF THE ROAD

THE glory has passed from the goldenrod's plume,
The purple-hued asters still linger in bloom
The birch is bright yellow, the sumachs are red,
The maples like torches aflame overhead.

But what if the joy of the summer is past,
And winter's wild herald is blowing his blast?
For me dull November is sweeter than May,
For my love is its sunshine,—she meets me to-day!

Will she come? Will the ring-dove return to her nest?
Will the needle swing back from the east or the west?
At the stroke of the hour she will be at her gate;
A friend may prove laggard,—love never comes late.

Do I see her afar in the distance? Not yet.
Too early! Too early! She could not forget!
When I cross the old bridge where the brook overflowed,
She will flash full in sight at the turn of the road.

I pass the low wall where the ivy entwines;
I tread the brown pathway that leads through the pines;
I haste by the boulder that lies in the field,
Where her promise at parting was lovingly sealed.

Will she come by the hillside or round through the wood?
Will she wear her brown dress or her mantle and hood?
The minute draws near,—but her watch may go wrong;
My heart will be asking, What keeps her so long?

Why doubt for a moment? More shame if I do!
Why question? Why tremble? Are angels more true?
She would come to the lover who calls her his own
Though she trod in the track of a whirling cyclone!

I crossed the old bridge ere the minute had passed.
I looked: lo! my Love stood before me at last.
Her eyes, how they sparkled, her cheeks, how they glowed,
As we met, face to face, at the turn of the road!

IN VITA MINERVA

VEX not the Muse with idle prayers, —
She will not hear thy call;
She steals upon thee unawares,
Or seeks thee not at all.

Soft as the moonbeams when they sought
Endymion's fragrant bower,
She parts the whispering leaves of thought
To show her full-blown flower.

For thee her wooing hour has passed,
The singing birds have flown,
And winter comes with icy blast
To chill thy buds unblown.

Yet, though the woods no longer thrill
As once their arches rung,
Sweet echoes hover round thee still
Of songs thy summer sung.

Live in thy past; await no more
The rush of heaven-sent wings;
Earth still has music left in store
While Memory sighs and sings.

READINGS OVER THE TEACUPS

FIVE STORIES AND A SEQUEL
TO MY OLD READERS

You know "The Teacups," that congenial set
Which round the Teapot you have often met;
The grave DICTATOR, him you knew of old,—
Knew as the shepherd of another fold
Grayer he looks, less youthful, but the same
As when you called him by a different name.
Near him the MISTRESS, whose experienced skill
Has taught her duly every cup to fill;
"Weak;" "strong;" "cool;" "lukewarm;" "hot as you can pour;"
"No sweetening;" "sugared;" "two lumps;" "one lump more."
Next, the PROFESSOR, whose scholastic phrase
At every turn the teacher's tongue betrays,
Trying so hard to make his speech precise
The captious listener finds it overnice.

Nor be forgotten our ANNEXES twain,
Nor HE, the owner of the squinting brain,
Which, while its curious fancies we pursue,
Oft makes us question, "Are we crack-brained too?"

Along the board our growing list extends,
As one by one we count our clustering friends,—
The youthful DOCTOR waiting for his share
Of fits and fevers when his crown gets bare;
In strong, dark lines our square-nibbed pen should draw
The lordly presence of the MAN OF LAW;
Our bashful TUTOR claims a humbler place,
A lighter touch, his slender form to trace.
Mark the fair lady he is seated by,—
Some say he is her lover,—some deny,—
Watch them together,—time alone can show
If dead-ripe friendship turns to love or no.

Where in my list of phrases shall I seek
The fitting words of NUMBER FIVE to speak?
Such task demands a readier pen than mine,—
What if I steal the Tutor's Valentine?

Why should I call her gracious, winning, fair?
Why with the loveliest of her sex compare?
Those varied charms have many a Muse inspired,—
At last their worn superlatives have tired;
Wit, beauty, sweetness, each alluring grace,
All these in honeyed verse have found their place;
I need them not,—two little words I find
Which hold them all in happiest form combined;
No more with baffled language will I strive,—
All in one breath I utter: Number Five!

Now count our teaspoons—if you care to learn
How many tinkling cups were served in turn,—
Add all together, you will find them ten,—
Our young MUSICIAN joined us now and then.
Our bright DELILAH you must needs recall,
The comely handmaid, youngest of us all;
Need I remind you how the little maid
Came at a pinch to our Professor's aid,—
Trimmed his long locks with unrelenting shears
And eased his looks of half a score of years?

Sometimes, at table, as you well must know,
The stream of talk will all at once run low,
The air seems smitten with a sudden chill,
The wit grows silent and the gossip still;
This was our poet's chance, the hour of need,
When rhymes and stories we were used to read.
One day a whisper round the teacups stole,—
"No scrap of paper in the silver bowl!"
(Our "poet's corner" may I not expect
My kindly reader still may recollect?)
"What! not a line to keep our souls alive?"
Spoke in her silvery accents Number Five.
"No matter, something we must find to read,—
Find it or make it,—yes, we must indeed!
Now I remember I have seen at times
Some curious stories in a book of rhymes,—
How certain secrets, long in silence sealed,

In after days were guessed at or revealed.
Those stories, doubtless, some of you must know,—
They all were written many a year ago;
But an old story, be it false or true,
Twice told, well told, is twice as good as new;
Wait but three sips and I will go myself,
And fetch the book of verses from its shelf."
No time was lost in finding what she sought,—
Gone but one moment,—lo! the book is brought.

"Now, then, Professor, fortune has decreed
That you, this evening, shall be first to read,—
Lucky for us that listen, for in fact
Who reads this poem must know how to *act* ."
Right well she knew that in his greener age
He had a mighty hankering for the stage.
The patient audience had not long to wait;
Pleased with his chance, he smiled and took the bait;
Through his wild hair his coaxing fingers ran,—
He spread the page before him and began.

THE BANKER'S SECRET

THE Banker's dinner is the stateliest feast
The town has heard of for a year, at least;
The sparry lustres shed their broadest blaze,
Damask and silver catch and spread the rays;
The florist's triumphs crown the daintier spoil
Won from the sea, the forest, or the soil;
The steaming hot-house yields its largest pines,
The sunless vaults unearth their oldest wines;
With one admiring look the scene survey,
And turn a moment from the bright display.

Of all the joys of earthly pride or power,
What gives most life, worth living, in an hour?
When Victory settles on the doubtful fight
And the last foeman wheels in panting flight,
No thrill like this is felt beneath the sun;
Life's sovereign moment is a battle won.
But say what next? To shape a Senate's choice,
By the strong magic of the master's voice;
To ride the stormy tempest of debate
That whirls the wavering fortunes of the state.
Third in the list, the happy lover's prize
Is won by honeyed words from women's eyes.
If some would have it first instead of third,
So let it be, — I answer not a word.
The fourth, — sweet readers, let the thoughtless half
Have its small shrug and inoffensive laugh;
Let the grave quarter wear its virtuous frown,
The stern half-quarter try to scowl us down;
But the last eighth, the choice and sifted few,
Will hear my words, and, pleased, confess them true.

Among the great whom Heaven has made to shine,
How few have learned the art of arts, — to dine!
Nature, indulgent to our daily need,

Kind-hearted mother! taught us all to feed;
But the chief art,—how rarely Nature flings
This choicest gift among her social kings
Say, man of truth, has life a brighter hour
Than waits the chosen guest who knows his power?
He moves with ease, itself an angel charm,—
Lifts with light touch my lady's jewelled arm,
Slides to his seat, half leading and half led,
Smiling but quiet till the grace is said,
Then gently kindles, while by slow degrees
Creep softly out the little arts that please;
Bright looks, the cheerful language of the eye,
The neat, crisp question and the gay reply,—
Talk light and airy, such as well may pass
Between the rested fork and lifted glass;—
With play like this the earlier evening flies,
Till rustling silks proclaim the ladies rise.
His hour has come,—he looks along the chairs,
As the Great Duke surveyed his iron squares.
That's the young traveller,—is n't much to show,—
Fast on the road, but at the table slow.
Next him,—you see the author in his look,—
His forehead lined with wrinkles like a book,—
Wrote the great history of the ancient Huns,—
Holds back to fire among the heavy guns.
Oh, there's our poet seated at his side,
Beloved of ladies, soft, cerulean-eyed.
Poets are prosy in their common talk,
As the fast trotters, for the most part, walk.
And there's our well-dressed gentleman, who sits,
By right divine, no doubt, among the wits,
Who airs his tailor's patterns when he walks,
The man that often speaks, but never talks.
Why should he talk, whose presence lends a grace
To every table where he shows his face?
He knows the manual of the silver fork,
Can name his claret—if he sees the cork,—
Remark that "White-top" was considered fine,
But swear the "Juno" is the better wine;—
Is not this talking? Ask Quintilian's rules;
If they say No, the town has many fools.
Pause for a moment,—for our eyes behold

The plain unsceptred king, the man of gold,
The thrice illustrious threefold millionnaire;
Mark his slow-creeping, dead, metallic stare;
His eyes, dull glimmering, like the balance-pan
That weighs its guinea as he weighs his man.
Who's next? An artist in a satin tie
Whose ample folds defeat the curious eye.
And there 's the cousin,—must be asked, you know,—
Looks like a spinster at a baby-show.
Hope he is cool,—they set him next the door,—
And likes his place, between the gap and bore.
Next comes a Congressman, distinguished guest
We don't count him,—they asked him with the rest;
And then some white cravats, with well-shaped ties,
And heads above them which their owners prize.

     Of all that cluster round the genial board,
Not one so radiant as the banquet's lord.
Some say they fancy, but they know not why,
A shade of trouble brooding in his eye,
Nothing, perhaps,—the rooms are overhot,—
Yet see his cheek,—the dull-red burning spot,—
Taste the brown sherry which he does not pass,—
Ha! That is brandy; see him fill his glass!
But not forgetful of his feasting friends,
To each in turn some lively word he sends;
See how he throws his baited lines about,
And plays his men as anglers play their trout.
A question drops among the listening crew
And hits the traveller, pat on Timbuctoo.
We're on the Niger, somewhere near its source,—
Not the least hurry, take the river's course
Through Kissi, Foota, Kankan, Bammakoo,
Bambarra, Sego, so to Timbuctoo,
Thence down to Youri;—stop him if we can,
We can't fare worse,—wake up the Congressman!
The Congressman, once on his talking legs,
Stirs up his knowledge to its thickest dregs;
Tremendous draught for dining men to quaff!
Nothing will choke him but a purpling laugh.
A word,—a shout,—a mighty roar,—'t is done;
Extinguished; lassoed by a treacherous pun.

A laugh is priming to the loaded soul;
The scattering shots become a steady roll,
Broke by sharp cracks that run along the line,
The light artillery of the talker's wine.
The kindling goblets flame with golden dews,
The hoarded flasks their tawny fire diffuse,
And the Rhine's breast-milk gushes cold and bright,
Pale as the moon and maddening as her light;
With crimson juice the thirsty southern sky
Sucks from the hills where buried armies lie,
So that the dreamy passion it imparts
Is drawn from heroes' bones and lovers' hearts.
But lulls will come; the flashing soul transmits
Its gleams of light in alternating fits.
The shower of talk that rattled down amain
Ends in small patterings like an April's rain;

With the dry sticks all bonfires are begun;
Bring the first fagot, proser number one
The voices halt; the game is at a stand;
Now for a solo from the master-hand
'T is but a story, — quite a simple thing, —
An aria touched upon a single string,
But every accent comes with such a grace
The stupid servants listen in their place,
Each with his waiter in his lifted hands,
Still as a well-bred pointer when he stands.
A query checks him: "Is he quite exact?"
(This from a grizzled, square-jawed man of fact.)
The sparkling story leaves him to his fate,
Crushed by a witness, smothered with a date,
As a swift river, sown with many a star,
Runs brighter, rippling on a shallow bar.
The smooth divine suggests a graver doubt;
A neat quotation bowls the parson out;
Then, sliding gayly from his own display,
He laughs the learned dulness all away.
So, with the merry tale and jovial song,
The jocund evening whirls itself along,
Till the last chorus shrieks its loud encore,
And the white neckcloths vanish through the door.

One savage word! — The menials know its tone,
And slink away; the master stands alone.

"Well played, by —-"; breathe not what were best unheard;
His goblet shivers while he speaks the word,—
"If wine tells truth,—and so have said the wise,—
It makes me laugh to think how brandy lies!
Bankrupt to-morrow,—millionnaire to-day,—
The farce is over,—now begins the play!"
The spring he touches lets a panel glide;
An iron closet harks beneath the slide,
Bright with such treasures as a search might bring
From the deep pockets of a truant king.
Two diamonds, eyeballs of a god of bronze,
Bought from his faithful priest, a pious bonze;
A string of brilliants; rubies, three or four;
Bags of old coin and bars of virgin ore;
A jewelled poniard and a Turkish knife,
Noiseless and useful if we come to strife.
Gone! As a pirate flies before the wind,
And not one tear for all he leaves behind
From all the love his better years have known
Fled like a felon,—ah! but not alone!
The chariot flashes through a lantern's glare,—
Oh the wild eyes! the storm of sable hair!
Still to his side the broken heart will cling,—
The bride of shame, the wife without the ring
Hark, the deep oath,—the wail of frenzied woe,—
Lost! lost to hope of Heaven and peace below!

    He kept his secret; but the seed of crime
Bursts of itself in God's appointed time.
The lives he wrecked were scattered far and wide;
One never blamed nor wept,—she only died.
None knew his lot, though idle tongues would say
He sought a lonely refuge far away,
And there, with borrowed name and altered mien,
He died unheeded, as he lived unseen.
The moral market had the usual chills
Of Virtue suffering from protested bills;
The White Cravats, to friendship's memory true,
Sighed for the past, surveyed the future too;
Their sorrow breathed in one expressive line,—
"Gave pleasant dinners; who has got his wine?"

. . . .

The reader paused,—the Teacups knew his ways,—
He, like the rest, was not averse to praise.
Voices and hands united; every one
Joined in approval: "Number Three, well done!"

"Now for the Exile's story; if my wits
Are not at fault, his curious record fits
Neatly as sequel to the tale we've heard;
Not wholly wild the fancy, nor absurd
That this our island hermit well might be
That story's hero, fled from over sea.
Come, Number Seven, we would not have you strain
The fertile powers of that inventive brain.
Read us 'The Exile's Secret'; there's enough
Of dream-like fiction and fantastic stuff
In the strange web of mystery that invests
The lonely isle where sea birds build their nests."

"Lies! naught but lies!" so Number Seven began,—
No harm was known of that secluded man.
He lived alone,—who would n't if he might,
And leave the rogues and idiots out of sight?
A foolish story,—still, I'll do my best,—
The house was real,—don't believe the rest.
How could a ruined dwelling last so long
Without its legends shaped in tale and song?
Who was this man of whom they tell the lies?
Perhaps—why not?—NAPOLEON! in disguise,—
So some said, kidnapped from his ocean coop,
Brought to this island in a coasting sloop,—
Meanwhile a sham Napoleon in his place
Played Nap. and saved Sir Hudson from disgrace.
Such was one story; others used to say,
"No,—not Napoleon,—it was Marshal Ney."
"Shot?" Yes, no doubt, but not with balls of lead,
But balls of pith that never shoot folks dead.
He wandered round, lived South for many a year,
At last came North and fixed his dwelling here.
Choose which you will of all the tales that pile
Their mingling fables on the tree-crowned isle.
Who wrote this modest version I suppose
That truthful Teacup, our Dictator, knows;
Made up of various legends, it would seem,

The sailor's yarn, the crazy poet's dream.
Such tales as this, by simple souls received,
At first are stared at and at last believed;
From threads like this the grave historians try
To weave their webs, and never know they lie.
Hear, then, the fables that have gathered round
The lonely home an exiled stranger found.

THE EXILE'S SECRET

YE that have faced the billows and the spray
Of good St. Botolph's island-studded bay,
As from the gliding bark your eye has scanned
The beaconed rocks, the wave-girt hills of sand,
Have ye not marked one elm-o'ershadowed isle,
Round as the dimple chased in beauty's smile, —
A stain of verdure on an azure field,
Set like a jewel in a battered shield?
Fixed in the narrow gorge of Ocean's path,
Peaceful it meets him in his hour of wrath;
When the mailed Titan, scourged by hissing gales,
Writhes in his glistening coat of clashing scales,
The storm-beat island spreads its tranquil green,
Calm as an emerald on an angry queen.
So fair when distant should be fairer near;
A boat shall waft us from the outstretched pier.
The breeze blows fresh; we reach the island's edge,
Our shallop rustling through the yielding sedge.
No welcome greets us on the desert isle;
Those elms, far-shadowing, hide no stately pile
Yet these green ridges mark an ancient road;
And to! the traces of a fair abode;
The long gray line that marks a garden-wall,
And heaps of fallen beams, — fire-branded all.

Who sees unmoved, a ruin at his feet,
The lowliest home where human hearts have beat?
Its hearthstone, shaded with the bistre stain
A century's showery torrents wash in vain;
Its starving orchard, where the thistle blows
And mossy trunks still mark the broken rows;
Its chimney-loving poplar, oftenest seen
Next an old roof, or where a roof has been;
Its knot-grass, plantain, — all the social weeds,

Man's mute companions, following where he leads;
Its dwarfed, pale flowers, that show their straggling heads,
Sown by the wind from grass-choked garden-beds;
Its woodbine, creeping where it used to climb;
Its roses, breathing of the olden time;
All the poor shows the curious idler sees,
As life's thin shadows waste by slow degrees,
Till naught remains, the saddening tale to tell,
Save home's last wrecks, — the cellar and the well?

And whose the home that strews in black decay
The one green-glowing island of the bay?
Some dark-browed pirate's, jealous of the fate
That seized the strangled wretch of "Nix's Mate"?
Some forger's, skulking in a borrowed name,
Whom Tyburn's dangling halter yet may claim?
Some wan-eyed exile's, wealth and sorrow's heir,
Who sought a lone retreat for tears and prayer?
Some brooding poet's, sure of deathless fame,
Had not his epic perished in the flame?
Or some gray wooer's, whom a girlish frown
Chased from his solid friends and sober town?
Or some plain tradesman's, fond of shade and ease,
Who sought them both beneath these quiet trees?
Why question mutes no question can unlock,
Dumb as the legend on the Dighton rock?
One thing at least these ruined heaps declare, —
They were a shelter once; a man lived there.

But where the charred and crumbling records fail,
Some breathing lips may piece the half-told tale;
No man may live with neighbors such as these,
Though girt with walls of rock and angry seas,
And shield his home, his children, or his wife,
His ways, his means, his vote, his creed, his life,
From the dread sovereignty of Ears and Eyes
And the small member that beneath them lies.
They told strange things of that mysterious man;
Believe who will, deny them such as can;
Why should we fret if every passing sail
Had its old seaman talking on the rail?
The deep-sunk schooner stuffed with Eastern lime,
Slow wedging on, as if the waves were slime;

The knife-edged clipper with her ruffled spars,
The pawing steamer with her inane of stars,
The bull-browed galliot butting through the stream,
The wide-sailed yacht that slipped along her beam,
The deck-piled sloops, the pinched chebacco-boats,
The frigate, black with thunder-freighted throats,
All had their talk about the lonely man;
And thus, in varying phrase, the story ran.
His name had cost him little care to seek,
Plain, honest, brief, a decent name to speak,
Common, not vulgar, just the kind that slips
With least suggestion from a stranger's lips.
His birthplace England, as his speech might show,
Or his hale cheek, that wore the red-streak's glow;
His mouth sharp-moulded; in its mirth or scorn
There came a flash as from the milky corn,
When from the ear you rip the rustling sheath,
And the white ridges show their even teeth.
His stature moderate, but his strength confessed,
In spite of broadcloth, by his ample breast;
Full-armed, thick-handed; one that had been strong,
And might be dangerous still, if things went wrong.
He lived at ease beneath his elm-trees' shade,
Did naught for gain, yet all his debts were paid;
Rich, so 't was thought, but careful of his store;
Had all he needed, claimed to have no more.

But some that lingered round the isle at night
Spoke of strange stealthy doings in their sight;
Of creeping lonely visits that he made
To nooks and corners, with a torch and spade.
Some said they saw the hollow of a cave;
One, given to fables, swore it was a grave;
Whereat some shuddered, others boldly cried,
Those prowling boatmen lied, and knew they lied.
They said his house was framed with curious cares,
Lest some old friend might enter unawares;
That on the platform at his chamber's door
Hinged a loose square that opened through the floor;
Touch the black silken tassel next the bell,
Down, with a crash, the flapping trap-door fell;
Three stories deep the falling wretch would strike,

To writhe at leisure on a boarder's pike.
By day armed always; double-armed at night,

His tools lay round him; wake him such as might.
A carbine hung beside his India fan,
His hand could reach a Turkish ataghan;
Pistols, with quaint-carved stocks and barrels gilt,
Crossed a long dagger with a jewelled hilt;
A slashing cutlass stretched along the bed; —
All this was what those lying boatmen said.
Then some were full of wondrous stories told
Of great oak chests and cupboards full of gold;
Of the wedged ingots and the silver bars
That cost old pirates ugly sabre-scars;
How his laced wallet often would disgorge
The fresh-faced guinea of an English George,
Or sweated ducat, palmed by Jews of yore,
Or double Joe, or Portuguese moidore;
And how his finger wore a rubied ring
Fit for the white-necked play-girl of a king.
But these fine legends, told with staring eyes,
Met with small credence from the old and wise.

Why tell each idle guess, each whisper vain?
Enough: the scorched and cindered beams remain.
He came, a silent pilgrim to the West,
Some old-world mystery throbbing in his breast;
Close to the thronging mart he dwelt alone;
He lived; he died. The rest is all unknown.

Stranger, whose eyes the shadowy isle survey,
As the black steamer dashes through the bay,
Why ask his buried secret to divine?
He was thy brother; speak, and tell us thine!

. . . .

Silence at first, a kind of spell-bound pause;
Then all the Teacups tinkled their applause;
When that was hushed no sound the stillness broke
Till once again the soft-voiced lady spoke:

"The Lover's Secret, — surely that must need
The youngest voice our table holds to read.
Which of our two 'Annexes' shall we choose?
Either were charming, neither will refuse;

But choose we must,—what better can we do
Than take the younger of the youthful two?"

True to the primal instinct of her sex,
"Why, that means me," half whispered each Annex.
"What if it does?" the voiceless question came,
That set those pale New England cheeks aflame;
"Our old-world scholar may have ways to teach
Of Oxford English, Britain's purest speech,—
She shall be youngest,—youngest for *to-day* ,—
Our dates we'll fix hereafter as we may;
All rights reserved ,—the words we know so well,
That guard the claims of books which never sell."
The British maiden bowed a pleased assent,
Her two long ringlets swinging as she bent;
The glistening eyes her eager soul looked through
Betrayed her lineage in their Saxon blue.
Backward she flung each too obtrusive curl
And thus began,—the rose-lipped English girl.

THE LOVER'S SECRET

WHAT ailed young Lucius? Art had vainly tried
To guess his ill, and found herself defied.
The Augur plied his legendary skill;
Useless; the fair young Roman languished still.
His chariot took him every cloudless day
Along the Pincian Hill or Appian Way;
They rubbed his wasted limbs with sulphurous oil,
Oozed from the far-off Orient's heated soil;
They led him tottering down the steamy path
Where bubbling fountains filled the thermal bath;
Borne in his litter to Egeria's cave,
They washed him, shivering, in her icy wave.
They sought all curious herbs and costly stones,
They scraped the moss that grew on dead men's bones,
They tried all cures the votive tablets taught,
Scoured every place whence healing drugs were brought,
O'er Thracian hills his breathless couriers ran,
His slaves waylaid the Syrian caravan.
At last a servant heard a stranger speak
A new chirurgeon's name; a clever Greek,
Skilled in his art; from Pergamus he came
To Rome but lately; GALEN was the name.

The Greek was called: a man with piercing eyes,
Who must be cunning, and who might be wise.
He spoke but little,—if they pleased, he said,
He 'd wait awhile beside the sufferer's bed.
So by his side he sat, serene and calm,
His very accents soft as healing balm;
Not curious seemed, but every movement spied,
His sharp eyes searching where they seemed to glide;
Asked a few questions,—what he felt, and where?
"A pain just here," "A constant beating there."
Who ordered bathing for his aches and ails?
"Charmis, the water-doctor from Marseilles."
What was the last prescription in his case?
"A draught of wine with powdered chrysoprase."
Had he no secret grief he nursed alone?
A pause; a little tremor; answer,—"None."
Thoughtful, a moment, sat the cunning leech,
And muttered "Eros!" in his native speech.
In the broad atrium various friends await
The last new utterance from the lips of fate;
Men, matrons, maids, they talk the question o'er,
And, restless, pace the tessellated floor.
Not unobserved the youth so long had pined
By gentle-hearted dames and damsels kind;
One with the rest, a rich Patrician's pride,
The lady Hermia, called "the golden-eyed";
The same the old Proconsul fain must woo,
Whom, one dark night, a masked sicarius slew;
The same black Crassus over roughly pressed
To hear his suit,—the Tiber knows the rest.
(Crassus was missed next morning by his set;
Next week the fishers found him in their net.)
She with the others paced the ample hall,
Fairest, alas! and saddest of them all.

At length the Greek declared, with puzzled face,
Some strange enchantment mingled in the case,
And naught would serve to act as counter-charm
Save a warm bracelet from a maiden's arm.
Not every maiden's,—many might be tried;
Which not in vain, experience must decide.
Were there no damsels willing to attend

And do such service for a suffering friend?
The message passed among the waiting crowd,
First in a whisper, then proclaimed aloud.
Some wore no jewels; some were disinclined,
For reasons better guessed at than defined;
Though all were saints,—at least professed to be,—
The list all counted, there were named but three.
The leech, still seated by the patient's side,
Held his thin wrist, and watched him, eagle-eyed.
Aurelia first, a fair-haired Tuscan girl,
Slipped off her golden asp, with eyes of pearl.
His solemn head the grave physician shook;
The waxen features thanked her with a look.
Olympia next, a creature half divine,
Sprung from the blood of old Evander's line,
Held her white arm, that wore a twisted chain
Clasped with an opal-sheeny cymophane.
In vain, O daughter I said the baffled Greek.
The patient sighed the thanks he could not speak.

Last, Hermia entered; look, that sudden start!
The pallium heaves above his leaping heart;
The beating pulse, the cheek's rekindled flame,
Those quivering lips, the secret all proclaim.
The deep disease long throbbing in the breast,
The dread enchantment, all at once confessed!
The case was plain; the treatment was begun;
And Love soon cured the mischief he had done.

Young Love, too oft thy treacherous bandage slips
Down from the eyes it blinded to the lips!
Ask not the Gods, O youth, for clearer sight,
But the bold heart to plead thy cause aright.
And thou, fair maiden, when thy lovers sigh,
Suspect thy flattering ear, but trust thine eye;
And learn this secret from the tale of old
No love so true as love that dies untold.

. . . .

"Bravo, Annex!" they shouted, every one,—
"Not Mrs. Kemble's self had better done."
"Quite so," she stammered in her awkward way,—
Not just the thing, but something she must say.

The teaspoon chorus tinkled to its close
When from his chair the MAN OF LAW arose,
Called by her voice whose mandate all obeyed,
And took the open volume she displayed.
Tall, stately, strong, his form begins to own
Some slight exuberance in its central zone,—
That comely fulness of the growing girth
Which fifty summers lend the sons of earth.
A smooth, round disk about whose margin stray,
Above the temples, glistening threads of gray;
Strong, deep-cut grooves by toilsome decades wrought
On brow and mouth, the battle-fields of thought;
A voice that lingers in the listener's ear,
Grave, calm, far-reaching, every accent clear,—
(Those tones resistless many a foreman knew
That shaped their verdict ere the twelve withdrew;)
A statesman's forehead, athlete's throat and jaw,
Such the proud semblance of the Man of Law.
His eye just lighted on the printed leaf,
Held as a practised pleader holds his brief.
One whispered softly from behind his cup,
"He does not read,—his book is wrong side up!
He knows the story that it holds by heart,—
So like his own! How well he'll act his part!"
Then all were silent; not a rustling fan
Stirred the deep stillness as the voice began.

THE STATESMAN'S SECRET

WHO of all statesmen is his country's pride,
Her councils' prompter and her leaders' guide?
He speaks; the nation holds its breath to hear;
He nods, and shakes the sunset hemisphere.
Born where the primal fount of Nature springs
By the rude cradles of her throneless kings,
In his proud eye her royal signet flames,
By his own lips her Monarch she proclaims.
Why name his countless triumphs, whom to meet
Is to be famous, envied in defeat?
The keen debaters, trained to brawls and strife,
Who fire one shot, and finish with the knife,
Tried him but once, and, cowering in their shame,
Ground their hacked blades to strike at meaner game.

The lordly chief, his party's central stay,
Whose lightest word a hundred votes obey,
Found a new listener seated at his side,
Looked in his eye, and felt himself defied,
Flung his rash gauntlet on the startled floor,
Met the all-conquering, fought,—and ruled no more.
See where he moves, what eager crowds attend!
What shouts of thronging multitudes ascend!
If this is life,—to mark with every hour
The purple deepening in his robes of power,
To see the painted fruits of honor fall
Thick at his feet, and choose among them all,
To hear the sounds that shape his spreading name
Peal through the myriad organ-stops of fame,
Stamp the lone isle that spots the seaman's chart,
And crown the pillared glory of the mart,
To count as peers the few supremely wise
Who mark their planet in the angels' eyes,—
If this is life—
What savage man is he
Who strides alone beside the sounding sea?
Alone he wanders by the murmuring shore,
His thoughts as restless as the waves that roar;
Looks on the sullen sky as stormy-browed
As on the waves yon tempest-brooding cloud,
Heaves from his aching breast a wailing sigh,
Sad as the gust that sweeps the clouded sky.
Ask him his griefs; what midnight demons plough
The lines of torture on his lofty brow;
Unlock those marble lips, and bid them speak
The mystery freezing in his bloodless cheek.
His secret? Hid beneath a flimsy word;
One foolish whisper that ambition heard;
And thus it spake: "Behold yon gilded chair,
The world's one vacant throne,—thy plate is there!"

Ah, fatal dream! What warning spectres meet
In ghastly circle round its shadowy seat!
Yet still the Tempter murmurs in his ear
The maddening taunt he cannot choose but hear
"Meanest of slaves, by gods and men accurst,
He who is second when he might be first

Climb with bold front the ladder's topmost round,
Or chain thy creeping footsteps to the ground!"
Illustrious Dupe! Have those majestic eyes
Lost their proud fire for such a vulgar prize?
Art thou the last of all mankind to know
That party-fights are won by aiming low?
Thou, stamped by Nature with her royal sign,
That party-hirelings hate a look like thine?
Shake from thy sense the wild delusive dream
Without the purple, art thou not supreme?
And soothed by love unbought, thy heart shall own
A nation's homage nobler than its throne!

. . . .

Loud rang the plaudits; with them rose the thought,
"Would he had learned the lesson he has taught!"
Used to the tributes of the noisy crowd,
The stately speaker calmly smiled and bowed;
The fire within a flushing cheek betrayed,
And eyes that burned beneath their penthouse shade.

"The clock strikes ten, the hours are flying fast, —
Now, Number Five, we've kept you till the last!"

What music charms like those caressing tones
Whose magic influence every listener owns, —
Where all the woman finds herself expressed,
And Heaven's divinest effluence breathes confessed?
Such was the breath that wooed our ravished ears,
Sweet as the voice a dreaming vestal hears;
Soft as the murmur of a brooding dove,
It told the mystery of a mother's love.

THE MOTHER'S SECRET

How sweet the sacred legend—if unblamed
In my slight verse such holy things are named—
Of Mary's secret hours of hidden joy,
Silent, but pondering on her wondrous boy!
Ave, Maria! Pardon, if I wrong
Those heavenly words that shame my earthly song!
The choral host had closed the Angel's strain
Sung to the listening watch on Bethlehem's plain,
And now the shepherds, hastening on their way,

Sought the still hamlet where the Infant lay.
They passed the fields that gleaning Ruth toiled o'er,—
They saw afar the ruined threshing-floor
Where Moab's daughter, homeless and forlorn,
Found Boaz slumbering by his heaps of corn;
And some remembered how the holy scribe,
Skilled in the lore of every jealous tribe,
Traced the warm blood of Jesse's royal son
To that fair alien, bravely wooed and won.
So fared they on to seek the promised sign,
That marked the anointed heir of David's line.
At last, by forms of earthly semblance led,
They found the crowded inn, the oxen's shed.

No pomp was there, no glory shone around
On the coarse straw that strewed the reeking ground;
One dim retreat a flickering torch betrayed,—
In that poor cell the Lord of Life was laid
The wondering shepherds told their breathless tale
Of the bright choir that woke the sleeping vale;
Told how the skies with sudden glory flamed,
Told how the shining multitude proclaimed,
"Joy, joy to earth! Behold the hallowed morn
In David's city Christ the Lord is born!
'Glory to God!' let angels shout on high,
'Good-will to men!' the listening earth reply!"
They spoke with hurried words and accents wild;
Calm in his cradle slept the heavenly child.
No trembling word the mother's joy revealed,—
One sigh of rapture, and her lips were sealed;
Unmoved she saw the rustic train depart,
But kept their words to ponder in her heart.

Twelve years had passed; the boy was fair and tall,
Growing in wisdom, finding grace with all.
The maids of Nazareth, as they trooped to fill
Their balanced urns beside the mountain rill,
The gathered matrons, as they sat and spun,
Spoke in soft words of Joseph's quiet son.
No voice had reached the Galilean vale
Of star-led kings, or awe-struck shepherd's tale;
In the meek, studious child they only saw
The future Rabbi, learned in Israel's law.

Beyond the hills that girt the village green;
Save when at midnight, o'er the starlit sands,
Snatched from the steel of Herod's murdering bands,
A babe, close folded to his mother's breast,
Through Edom's wilds he sought the sheltering West.
Then Joseph spake: "Thy boy hath largely grown;
Weave him fine raiment, fitting to be shown;
Fair robes beseem the pilgrim, as the priest;
Goes he not with us to the holy feast?"
And Mary culled the flaxen fibres white;
Till eve she spun; she spun till morning light.
The thread was twined; its parting meshes through
From hand to hand her restless shuttle flew,
Till the full web was wound upon the beam;
Love's curious toil,—a vest without a seam!
They reach the Holy Place, fulfil the days
To solemn feasting given, and grateful praise.
At last they turn, and far Moriah's height
Melts in the southern sky and fades from sight.
All day the dusky caravan has flowed
In devious trails along the winding road;
(For many a step their homeward path attends,
And all the sons of Abraham are as friends.)
Evening has come,—the hour of rest and joy,—
Hush! Hush! That whisper,—"Where is Mary's boy?"
Oh, weary hour! Oh, aching days that passed
Filled with strange fears each wilder than the last,—
The soldier's lance, the fierce centurion's sword,
The crushing wheels that whirl some Roman lord,
The midnight crypt that sucks the captive's breath,
The blistering sun on Hinnom's vale of death!
Thrice on his cheek had rained the morning light;
Thrice on his lips the mildewed kiss of night,
Crouched by a sheltering column's shining plinth,
Or stretched beneath the odorous terebinth.
At last, in desperate mood, they sought once more
The Temple's porches, searched in vain before;
They found him seated with the ancient men,—
The grim old rufflers of the tongue and pen,—
Their bald heads glistening as they clustered near,
Their gray beards slanting as they turned to hear,
Lost in half-envious wonder and surprise

That lips so fresh should utter words so wise.
And Mary said,—as one who, tried too long,
Tells all her grief and half her sense of wrong,—
What is this thoughtless thing which thou hast done?
Lo, we have sought thee sorrowing, O my son!
Few words he spake, and scarce of filial tone,
Strange words, their sense a mystery yet unknown;
Then turned with them and left the holy hill,
To all their mild commands obedient still.
The tale was told to Nazareth's sober men,
And Nazareth's matrons told it oft again;
The maids retold it at the fountain's side,
The youthful shepherds doubted or denied;
It passed around among the listening friends,
With all that fancy adds and fiction lends,
Till newer marvels dimmed the young renown
Of Joseph's son, who talked the Rabbis down.

But Mary, faithful to its lightest word,
Kept in her heart the sayings she had heard,
Till the dread morning rent the Temple's veil,
And shuddering earth confirmed the wondrous tale.

Youth fades; love droops; the leaves of friendship fall
A mother's secret hope outlives them all.

. . . .

Hushed was the voice, but still its accents thrilled
The throbbing hearts its lingering sweetness filled.
The simple story which a tear repays
Asks not to share the noisy breath of praise.
A trance-like stillness,—scarce a whisper heard,
No tinkling teaspoon in its saucer stirred;
A deep-drawn sigh that would not be suppressed,
A sob, a lifted kerchief told the rest.

"Come now, Dictator," so the lady spoke,
"You too must fit your shoulder to the yoke;
You'll find there's something, doubtless, if you look,
To serve your purpose,—so, now take the book."
"Ah, my dear lady, you must know full well,
'Story, God bless you, I have none to tell.'
To those five stories which these pages hold
You all have listened,—every one is told.

There's nothing left to make you smile or weep,—
A few grave thoughts may work you off to sleep."

THE SECRET OF THE STARS

    Is man's the only throbbing heart that hides
The silent spring that feeds its whispering tides?
Speak from thy caverns, mystery-breeding Earth,
Tell the half-hinted story of thy birth,
And calm the noisy champions who have thrown
The book of types against the book of stone!

    Have ye not secrets, ye refulgent spheres,
No sleepless listener of the starlight hears?
In vain the sweeping equatorial pries
Through every world-sown corner of the skies,
To the far orb that so remotely strays
Our midnight darkness is its noonday blaze;
In vain the climbing soul of creeping man
Metes out the heavenly concave with a span,
Tracks into space the long-lost meteor's trail,
And weighs an unseen planet in the scale;
Still o'er their doubts the wan-eyed watchers sigh,
And Science lifts her still unanswered cry
"Are all these worlds, that speed their circling flight,
Dumb, vacant, soulless,—baubles of the night?
Warmed with God's smile and wafted by his breath,
To weave in ceaseless round the dance of Death?
Or rolls a sphere in each expanding zone,
Crowned with a life as varied as our own?"

    Maker of earth and stars! If thou hast taught
By what thy voice hath spoke, thy hand hath wrought,
By all that Science proves, or guesses true,
More than thy poet dreamed, thy prophet knew,—
The heavens still bow in darkness at thy feet,
And shadows veil thy cloud-pavilioned seat!
Not for ourselves we ask thee to reveal
One awful word beneath the future's seal;
What thou shalt tell us, grant us strength to bear;
What thou withholdest is thy single care.
Not for ourselves; the present clings too fast,
Moored to the mighty anchors of the past;
But when, with angry snap, some cable parts,

The sound re-echoing in our startled hearts, —
When, through the wall that clasps the harbor round,
And shuts the raving ocean from its bound,
Shattered and rent by sacrilegious hands,
The first mad billow leaps upon the sands, —
Then to the Future's awful page we turn,
And what we question hardly dare to learn.
Still let us hope! for while we seem to tread
The time-worn pathway of the nations dead,
Though Sparta laughs at all our warlike deeds,
And buried Athens claims our stolen creeds,
Though Rome, a spectre on her broken throne,
Beholds our eagle and recalls her own,
Though England fling her pennons on the breeze
And reign before us Mistress of the seas, —
While calm-eyed History tracks us circling round
Fate's iron pillar where they all were bound,
Still in our path a larger curve she finds,
The spiral widening as the chain unwinds
Still sees new beacons crowned with brighter flame
Than the old watch-fires, like, but not the same
No shameless haste shall spot with bandit-crime
Our destined empire snatched before its time.
Wait, — wait, undoubting, for the winds have caught
From our bold speech the heritage of thought;
No marble form that sculptured truth can wear
Vies with the image shaped in viewless air;
And thought unfettered grows through speech to deeds,
As the broad forest marches in its seeds.
What though we perish ere the day is won?
Enough to see its glorious work begun!
The thistle falls before a trampling clown,
But who can chain the flying thistle-down?
Wait while the fiery seeds of freedom fly,
The prairie blazes when the grass is dry!
What arms might ravish, leave to peaceful arts,
Wisdom and love shall win the roughest hearts;
So shall the angel who has closed for man
The blissful garden since his woes began

Swing wide the golden portals of the West,
And Eden's secret stand at length confessed!

. . . .

The reader paused; in truth he thought it time, —
Some threatening signs accused the drowsy rhyme.
The Mistress nodded, the Professor dozed,
The two Annexes sat with eyelids closed, —
Not sleeping, — no! But when one shuts one's eyes,
That one hears better no one, sure, denies.
The Doctor whispered in Delilah's ear,
Or seemed to whisper, for their heads drew near.
Not all the owner's efforts could restrain
The wild vagaries of the squinting brain, —
Last of the listeners Number Five alone
The patient reader still could call his own.

"Teacups, arouse!" 'T was thus the spell I broke;
The drowsy started and the slumberers woke.
"The sleep I promised you have now enjoyed,
Due to your hour of labor well employed.
Swiftly the busy moments have been passed;
This, our first 'Teacups,' must not be our last.
Here, on this spot, now consecrated ground,
The Order of 'The Teacups' let us found!
By winter's fireside and in summer's bower
Still shall it claim its ever-welcome hour,
In distant regions where our feet may roam
The magic teapot find or make a home;
Long may its floods their bright infusion pour,
Till time and teacups both shall be no more!"

VERSES FROM THE OLDEST PORTFOLIO

FROM THE "COLLEGIAN," 1830, ILLUSTRATED ANNUALS, ETC.

Nescit vox missa reverti.—Horat. Ars Poetica.
Ab lis qua non adjuvant quam mollissime oportet pedem
referre.—
Quintillian, L. VI. C. 4.

These verses have always been printed in my collected poems, and as the best of them may bear a single reading, I allow them to appear, but in a less conspicuous position than the other productions. A chick, before his shell is off his back, is hardly a fair subject for severe criticism. If one has written anything worth preserving, his first efforts may be objects of interest and curiosity. Other young authors may take encouragement from seeing how tame, how feeble, how commonplace were the rudimentary attempts of the half-fledged poet. If the boy or youth had anything in him, there will probably be some sign of it in the midst of his imitative mediocrities and ambitious failures. These "first verses" of mine, written before I was sixteen, have little beyond a common academy boy's ordinary performance. Yet a kindly critic said there was one line which showed a poetical quality:—

"The boiling ocean trembled into calm."

One of these poems—the reader may guess which—won fair words from Thackeray. The Spectre Pig was a wicked suggestion which came into my head after reading Dana's Buccaneer. Nobody seemed to find it out, and I never mentioned it to the venerable poet, who might not have been pleased with the parody. This is enough to say of these unvalued copies of verses.

FIRST VERSES

PHILLIPS ACADEMY, ANDOVER, MASS., 1824 OR 1825

TRANSLATION FROM THE ENEID, BOOK I.

THE god looked out upon the troubled deep
Waked into tumult from its placid sleep;

The flame of anger kindles in his eye
As the wild waves ascend the lowering sky;
He lifts his head above their awful height
And to the distant fleet directs his sight,
Now borne aloft upon the billow's crest,
Struck by the bolt or by the winds oppressed,
And well he knew that Juno's vengeful ire
Frowned from those clouds and sparkled in that fire.
On rapid pinions as they whistled by
He calls swift Zephyrus and Eurus nigh
Is this your glory in a noble line
To leave your confines and to ravage mine?
Whom I—but let these troubled waves subside—
Another tempest and I'll quell your pride!
Go—bear our message to your master's ear,
That wide as ocean I am despot here;
Let him sit monarch in his barren caves,
I wield the trident and control the waves
He said, and as the gathered vapors break
The swelling ocean seemed a peaceful lake;
To lift their ships the graceful nymphs essayed
And the strong trident lent its powerful aid;
The dangerous banks are sunk beneath the main,
And the light chariot skims the unruffled plain.
As when sedition fires the public mind,
And maddening fury leads the rabble blind,
The blazing torch lights up the dread alarm,
Rage points the steel and fury nerves the arm,
Then, if some reverend Sage appear in sight,
They stand—they gaze, and check their headlong flight,—
He turns the current of each wandering breast
And hushes every passion into rest,—
Thus by the power of his imperial arm
The boiling ocean trembled into calm;
With flowing reins the father sped his way
And smiled serene upon rekindled day.

THE MEETING OF THE DRYADS

Written after a general pruning of the trees around Harvard College. A little poem, on a similar occasion, may be found in the works of Swift, from which, perhaps, the idea was borrowed; although I was as much surprised as amused to meet with it some time after writing the following lines.

IT was not many centuries since,
When, gathered on the moonlit green,
Beneath the Tree of Liberty,
A ring of weeping sprites was seen.

The freshman's lamp had long been dim,
The voice of busy day was mute,
And tortured Melody had ceased
Her sufferings on the evening flute.

They met not as they once had met,
To laugh o'er many a jocund tale
But every pulse was beating low,
And every cheek was cold and pale.

There rose a fair but faded one,
Who oft had cheered them with her song;
She waved a mutilated arm,
And silence held the listening throng.

"Sweet friends," the gentle nymph began,
"From opening bud to withering leaf,
One common lot has bound us all,
In every change of joy and grief.

"While all around has felt decay,
We rose in ever-living prime,
With broader shade and fresher green,
Beneath the crumbling step of Time.

"When often by our feet has past
Some biped, Nature's walking whim,

Say, have we trimmed one awkward shape,
Or lopped away one crooked limb?

"Go on, fair Science; soon to thee
Shall. Nature yield her idle boast;
Her vulgar fingers formed a tree,
But thou halt trained it to a post.

"Go, paint the birch's silver rind,
And quilt the peach with softer down;
Up with the willow's trailing threads,
Off with the sunflower's radiant crown!

"Go, plant the lily on the shore,
And set the rose among the waves,
And bid the tropic bud unbind
Its silken zone in arctic caves;

"Bring bellows for the panting winds,
Hang up a lantern by the moon,
And give the nightingale a fife,
And lend the eagle a balloon!

"I cannot smile,—the tide of scorn,
That rolled through every bleeding vein,
Comes kindling fiercer as it flows
Back to its burning source again.

"Again in every quivering leaf
That moment's agony I feel,
When limbs, that spurned the northern blast,
Shrunk from the sacrilegious steel.

"A curse upon the wretch who dared
To crop us with his felon saw!
May every fruit his lip shall taste
Lie like a bullet in his maw.

"In every julep that he drinks,
May gout, and bile, and headache be;
And when he strives to calm his pain,
May colic mingle with his tea.

"May nightshade cluster round his path,
And thistles shoot, and brambles cling;
May blistering ivy scorch his veins,
And dogwood burn, and nettles sting.

"On him may never shadow fall,
When fever racks his throbbing brow,
And his last shilling buy a rope
To hang him on my highest bough!"

She spoke;—the morning's herald beam
Sprang from the bosom of the sea,
And every mangled sprite returned
In sadness to her wounded tree.

THE MYSTERIOUS VISITOR

THERE was a sound of hurrying feet,
A tramp on echoing stairs,
There was a rush along the aisles,—
It was the hour of prayers.

And on, like Ocean's midnight wave,
The current rolled along,
When, suddenly, a stranger form
Was seen amidst the throng.

He was a dark and swarthy man,
That uninvited guest;
A faded coat of bottle-green
Was buttoned round his breast.

There was not one among them all
Could say from whence he came;
Nor beardless boy, nor ancient man,
Could tell that stranger's name.

All silent as the sheeted dead,
In spite of sneer and frown,
Fast by a gray-haired senior's side
He sat him boldly down.

There was a look of horror flashed
From out the tutor's eyes;
When all around him rose to pray,
The stranger did not rise!

A murmur broke along the crowd,
The prayer was at an end;
With ringing heels and measured tread,
A hundred forms descend.

Through sounding aisle, o'er grating stair,
The long procession poured,

Till all were gathered on the seats
Around the Commons board.

That fearful stranger! down he sat,
Unasked, yet undismayed;
And on his lip a rising smile
Of scorn or pleasure played.

He took his hat and hung it up,
With slow but earnest air;
He stripped his coat from off his back,
And placed it on a chair.

Then from his nearest neighbor's side
A knife and plate he drew;
And, reaching out his hand again,
He took his teacup too.

How fled the sugar from the bowl
How sunk the azure cream!
They vanished like the shapes that float
Upon a summer's dream.

A long, long draught,—an outstretched hand,—
And crackers, toast, and tea,
They faded from the stranger's touch,
Like dew upon the sea.

Then clouds were dark on many a brow,
Fear sat upon their souls,
And, in a bitter agony,
They clasped their buttered rolls.

A whisper trembled through the crowd,
Who could the stranger be?
And some were silent, for they thought
A cannibal was he.

What if the creature should arise,—
For he was stout and tall,—
And swallow down a sophomore,
Coat, crow's-foot, cap, and all!

All sullenly the stranger rose;
They sat in mute despair;
He took his hat from off the peg,
His coat from off the chair.

Four freshmen fainted on the seat,
Six swooned upon the floor;
Yet on the fearful being passed,
And shut the chapel door.

There is full many a starving man,
That walks in bottle green,
But never more that hungry one
In Commons hall was seen.

Yet often at the sunset hour,
When tolls the evening bell,
The freshman lingers on the steps,
That frightful tale to tell.

THE TOADSTOOL

THERE 's a thing that grows by the fainting flower,
And springs in the shade of the lady's bower;
The lily shrinks, and the rose turns pale,
When they feel its breath in the summer gale,
And the tulip curls its leaves in pride,
And the blue-eyed violet starts aside;
But the lily may flaunt, and the tulip stare,
For what does the honest toadstool care?
She does not glow in a painted vest,
And she never blooms on the maiden's breast;
But she comes, as the saintly sisters do,
In a modest suit of a Quaker hue.
And, when the stars in the evening skies
Are weeping dew from their gentle eyes,
The toad comes out from his hermit cell,
The tale of his faithful love to tell.

Oh, there is light in her lover's glance,
That flies to her heart like a silver lance;
His breeches are made of spotted skin,
His jacket 'is tight, and his pumps are thin;
In a cloudless night you may hear his song,
As its pensive melody floats along,
And, if you will look by the moonlight fair,
The trembling form of the toad is there.

And he twines his arms round her slender stem,
In the shade of her velvet diadem;
But she turns away in her maiden shame,
And will not breathe on the kindling flame;
He sings at her feet through the live-long night,
And creeps to his cave at the break of light;
And whenever he comes to the air above,
His throat is swelling with baffled love.

THE SPECTRE PIG

A BALLAD

IT was the stalwart butcher man,
That knit his swarthy brow,
And said the gentle Pig must die,
And sealed it with a vow.

And oh! it was the gentle Pig
Lay stretched upon the ground,
And ah! it was the cruel knife
His little heart that found.

They took him then, those wicked men,
They trailed him all along;
They put a stick between his lips,
And through his heels a thong;

And round and round an oaken beam
A hempen cord they flung,
And, like a mighty pendulum,
All solemnly he swung!

Now say thy prayers, thou sinful man,
And think what thou hast done,
And read thy catechism well,
Thou bloody-minded one;

For if his sprite should walk by night,
It better were for thee,
That thou wert mouldering in the ground,
Or bleaching in the sea.

It was the savage butcher then,
That made a mock of sin,
And swore a very wicked oath,
He did not care a pin.

It was the butcher's youngest son,—
His voice was broke with sighs,

And with his pocket-handkerchief
He wiped his little eyes;

All young and ignorant was he,
But innocent and mild,
And, in his soft simplicity,
Out spoke the tender child:—

"Oh, father, father, list to me;
The Pig is deadly sick,
And men have hung him by his heels,
And fed him with a stick."

It was the bloody butcher then,
That laughed as he would die,
Yet did he soothe the sorrowing child,
And bid him not to cry;—

"Oh, Nathan, Nathan, what's a Pig,
That thou shouldst weep and wail?
Come, bear thee like a butcher's child,
And thou shalt have his tail!"

It was the butcher's daughter then,
So slender and so fair,
That sobbed as it her heart would break,
And tore her yellow hair;

And thus she spoke in thrilling tone,—
Fast fell the tear-drops big:—
"Ah! woe is me! Alas! Alas!
The Pig! The Pig! The Pig!"

Then did her wicked father's lips
Make merry with her woe,
And call her many a naughty name,
Because she whimpered so.

Ye need not weep, ye gentle ones,
In vain your tears are shed,
Ye cannot wash his crimson hand,
Ye cannot soothe the dead.

The bright sun folded on his breast
His robes of rosy flame,
And softly over all the west
The shades of evening came.

He slept, and troops of murdered Pigs
Were busy with his dreams;
Loud rang their wild, unearthly shrieks,
Wide yawned their mortal seams.

The clock struck twelve; the Dead hath heard;
He opened both his eyes,
And sullenly he shook his tail
To lash the feeding flies.

One quiver of the hempen cord, —
One struggle and one bound, —
With stiffened limb and leaden eye,
The Pig was on the ground.

And straight towards the sleeper's house
His fearful way he wended;
And hooting owl and hovering bat
On midnight wing attended.

Back flew the bolt, up rose the latch,
And open swung the door,
And little mincing feet were heard
Pat, pat along the floor.

Two hoofs upon the sanded floor,
And two upon the bed;
And they are breathing side by side,
The living and the dead!

"Now wake, now wake, thou butcher man!
What makes thy cheek so pale?
Take hold! take hold! thou dost not fear
To clasp a spectre's tail?"

Untwisted every winding coil;
The shuddering wretch took hold,
All like an icicle it seemed,
So tapering and so cold.

"Thou com'st with me, thou butcher man!" —
He strives to loose his grasp,
But, faster than the clinging vine,
Those twining spirals clasp;

And open, open swung the door,
And, fleeter than the wind,

The shadowy spectre swept before,
The butcher trailed behind.

Fast fled the darkness of the night,
And morn rose faint and dim;
They called full loud, they knocked full long,
They did not waken him.

Straight, straight towards that oaken beam,
A trampled pathway ran;
A ghastly shape was swinging there, —
It was the butcher man.

TO A CAGED LION

Poor conquered monarch! though that haughty glance
Still speaks thy courage unsubdued by time,
And in the grandeur of thy sullen tread
Lives the proud spirit of thy burning clime;—
Fettered by things that shudder at thy roar,
Torn from thy pathless wilds to pace this narrow floor!

Thou wast the victor, and all nature shrunk
Before the thunders of thine awful wrath;
The steel-armed hunter viewed thee from afar,
Fearless and trackless in thy lonely path!
The famished tiger closed his flaming eye,
And crouched and panted as thy step went by!

Thou art the vanquished, and insulting man
Bars thy broad bosom as a sparrow's wing;
His nerveless arms thine iron sinews bind,
And lead in chains the desert's fallen king;
Are these the beings that have dared to twine
Their feeble threads around those limbs of thine?

So must it be; the weaker, wiser race,
That wields the tempest and that rides the sea,
Even in the stillness of thy solitude
Must teach the lesson of its power to thee;
And thou, the terror of the trembling wild,
Must bow thy savage strength, the mockery of a child!

THE STAR AND THE WATER-LILY

THE sun stepped down from his golden throne.
And lay in the silent sea,
And the Lily had folded her satin leaves,
For a sleepy thing was she;
What is the Lily dreaming of?
Why crisp the waters blue?
See, see, she is lifting her varnished lid!
Her white leaves are glistening through!

The Rose is cooling his burning cheek
In the lap of the breathless tide;—
The Lily hath sisters fresh and fair,
That would lie by the Rose's side;
He would love her better than all the rest,
And he would be fond and true;—
But the Lily unfolded her weary lids,
And looked at the sky so blue.

Remember, remember, thou silly one,
How fast will thy summer glide,
And wilt thou wither a virgin pale,
Or flourish a blooming bride?
Oh, the Rose is old, and thorny, and cold,
"And he lives on earth," said she;
"But the Star is fair and he lives in the air,
And he shall my bridegroom be."

But what if the stormy cloud should come,
And ruffle the silver sea?
Would he turn his eye from the distant sky,
To smile on a thing like thee?
Oh no, fair Lily, he will not send
One ray from his far-off throne;
The winds shall blow and the waves shall flow,
And thou wilt be left alone.

There is not a leaf on the mountain-top,
Nor a drop of evening dew,
Nor a golden sand on the sparkling shore,
Nor a pearl in the waters blue,
That he has not cheered with his fickle smile,
And warmed with his faithless beam, —
And will he be true to a pallid flower,
That floats on the quiet stream?

Alas for the Lily! she would not heed,
But turned to the skies afar,
And bared her breast to the trembling ray
That shot from the rising star;
The cloud came over the darkened sky,
And over the waters wide
She looked in vain through the beating rain,
And sank in the stormy tide.

ILLUSTRATION OF A PICTURE

"A SPANISH GIRL IN REVERIE,"

SHE twirled the string of golden beads,
That round her neck was hung, —-
My grandsire's gift; the good old man
Loved girls when he was young;
And, bending lightly o'er the cord,
And turning half away,
With something like a youthful sigh,
Thus spoke the maiden gray: —

"Well, one may trail her silken robe,
And bind her locks with pearls,
And one may wreathe the woodland rose
Among her floating curls;
And one may tread the dewy grass,
And one the marble floor,
Nor half-hid bosom heave the less,
Nor broidered corset more!

"Some years ago, a dark-eyed girl
Was sitting in the shade, —
There's something brings her to my mind
In that young dreaming maid, —
And in her hand she held a flower,
A flower, whose speaking hue
Said, in the language of the heart,
'Believe the giver true.'

"And, as she looked upon its leaves,
The maiden made a vow
To wear it when the bridal wreath
Was woven for her brow;
She watched the flower, as, day by day,
The leaflets curled and died;

But he who gave it never came
To claim her for his bride.

    "Oh, many a summer's morning glow
Has lent the rose its ray,
And many a winter's drifting snow
Has swept its bloom away;
But she has kept that faithless pledge
To this, her winter hour,
And keeps it still, herself alone,
And wasted like the flower."

    Her pale lip quivered, and the light
Gleamed in her moistening eyes;—
I asked her how she liked the tints
In those Castilian skies?
"She thought them misty,—'t was perhaps
Because she stood too near;"
She turned away, and as she turned
I saw her wipe a tear.

A ROMAN AQUEDUCT

THE sun-browned girl, whose limbs recline
When noon her languid hand has laid
Hot on the green flakes of the pine,
Beneath its narrow disk of shade;

As, through the flickering noontide glare,
She gazes on the rainbow chain
Of arches, lifting once in air
The rivers of the Roman's plain; —

Say, does her wandering eye recall
The mountain-current's icy wave, —
Or for the dead one tear let fall,
Whose founts are broken by their grave?

From stone to stone the ivy weaves
Her braided tracery's winding veil,
And lacing stalks and tangled leaves
Nod heavy in the drowsy gale.

And lightly floats the pendent vine,
That swings beneath her slender bow,
Arch answering arch, — whose rounded line
Seems mirrored in the wreath below.

How patient Nature smiles at Fame!
The weeds, that strewed the victor's way,
Feed on his dust to shroud his name,
Green where his proudest towers decay.

See, through that channel, empty now,
The scanty rain its tribute pours, —
Which cooled the lip and laved the brow
Of conquerors from a hundred shores.

Thus bending o'er the nation's bier,
Whose wants the captive earth supplied,
The dew of Memory's passing tear
Falls on the arches of her pride!

FROM A BACHELOR'S PRIVATE JOURNAL

SWEET Mary, I have never breathed
The love it were in vain to name;
Though round my heart a serpent wreathed,
I smiled, or strove to smile, the same.

Once more the pulse of Nature glows
With faster throb and fresher fire,
While music round her pathway flows,
Like echoes from a hidden lyre.

And is there none with me to share
The glories of the earth and sky?
The eagle through the pathless air
Is followed by one burning eye.

Ah no! the cradled flowers may wake,
Again may flow the frozen sea,
From every cloud a star may break,—
There conies no second spring to me.

Go,—ere the painted toys of youth
Are crushed beneath the tread of years;
Ere visions have been chilled to truth,
And hopes are washed away in tears.

Go,—for I will not bid thee weep,—
Too soon my sorrows will be thine,
And evening's troubled air shall sweep
The incense from the broken shrine.

If Heaven can hear the dying tone
Of chords that soon will cease to thrill,
The prayer that Heaven has heard alone
May bless thee when those chords are still.

LA GRISETTE

As Clemence! when I saw thee last
Trip down the Rue de Seine,
And turning, when thy form had past,
I said, "We meet again," —
I dreamed not in that idle glance
Thy latest image came,
And only left to memory's trance
A shadow and a name.

The few strange words my lips had taught
Thy timid voice to speak,
Their gentler signs, which often brought
Fresh roses to thy cheek,
The trailing of thy long loose hair
Bent o'er my couch of pain,
All, all returned, more sweet, more fair;
Oh, had we met again!

I walked where saint and virgin keep
The vigil lights of Heaven,
I knew that thou hadst woes to weep,
And sins to be forgiven;
I watched where Genevieve was laid,
I knelt by Mary's shrine,
Beside me low, soft voices prayed;
Alas! but where was thine?

And when the morning sun was bright,
When wind and wave were calm,
And flamed, in thousand-tinted light,
The rose of Notre Dame,

I wandered through the haunts of men,
From Boulevard to Quai,
Till, frowning o'er Saint Etienne,
The Pantheon's shadow lay.

  In vain, in vain; we meet no more,
Nor dream what fates befall;
And long upon the stranger's shore
My voice on thee may call,
When years have clothed the line in moss
That tells thy name and days,
And withered, on thy simple cross,
The wreaths of Pere-la-Chaise!

OUR YANKEE GIRLS

LET greener lands and bluer skies,
If such the wide earth shows,
With fairer cheeks and brighter eyes,
Match us the star and rose;
The winds that lift the Georgian's veil,
Or wave Circassia's curls,
Waft to their shores the sultan's sail,—
Who buys our Yankee girls?

The gay grisette, whose fingers touch
Love's thousand chords so well;
The dark Italian, loving much,
But more than one can tell;
And England's fair-haired, blue-eyed dame,
Who binds her brow with pearls;—
Ye who have seen them, can they shame
Our own sweet Yankee girls?

And what if court or castle vaunt
Its children loftier born?—
Who heeds the silken tassel's flaunt
Beside the golden corn?
They ask not for the dainty toil
Of ribboned knights and earls,
The daughters of the virgin soil,
Our freeborn Yankee girls!

By every hill whose stately pines
Wave their dark arms above
The home where some fair being shines,
To warm the wilds with love,
From barest rock to bleakest shore
Where farthest sail unfurls,
That stars and stripes are streaming o'er,—
God bless our Yankee girls!

L'INCONNUE

Is thy name Mary, maiden fair?
Such should, methinks, its music be;
The sweetest name that mortals bear
Were best befitting thee;
And she to whom it once was given,
Was half of earth and half of heaven.

I hear thy voice, I see thy smile,
I look upon thy folded hair;
Ah! while we dream not they beguile,
Our hearts are in the snare;
And she who chains a wild bird's wing
Must start not if her captive sing.

So, lady, take the leaf that falls,
To all but thee unseen, unknown;
When evening shades thy silent walls,
Then read it all alone;
In stillness read, in darkness seal,
Forget, despise, but not reveal!

STANZAS

STRANGE! that one lightly whispered tone
Is far, far sweeter unto me,
Than all the sounds that kiss the earth,
Or breathe along the sea;
But, lady, when thy voice I greet,
Not heavenly music seems so sweet.

I look upon the fair blue skies,
And naught but empty air I see;
But when I turn me to thin eyes,
It seemeth unto me
Ten thousand angels spread their wings
Within those little azure rings.

The lily bath the softest leaf
That ever western breeze bath fanned,
But thou shalt have the tender flower,
So I may take thy hand;
That little hand to me doth yield
More joy than all the broidered field.

O lady! there be many things
That seem right fair, below, above;
But sure not one among them all
Is half so sweet as love;—
Let us not pay our vows alone,
But join two altars both in one.

LINES BY A CLERK

OH! I did love her dearly,
And gave her toys and rings,
And I thought she meant sincerely,
When she took my pretty things.
But her heart has grown as icy
As a fountain in the fall,
And her love, that was so spicy,
It did not last at all.

I gave her once a locket,
It was filled with my own hair,
And she put it in her pocket
With very special care.
But a jeweller has got it, —
He offered it to me, —
And another that is not it
Around her neck I see.

For my cooings and my billings
I do not now complain,
But my dollars and my shillings
Will never come again;
They were earned with toil and sorrow,
But I never told her that,
And now I have to borrow,
And want another hat.

Think, think, thou cruel Emma,
When thou shalt hear my woe,
And know my sad dilemma,
That thou hast made it so.
See, see my beaver rusty,
Look, look upon this hole,
This coat is dim and dusty;
Oh let it rend thy soul!

Before the gates of fashion
I daily bent my knee,
But I sought the shrine of passion,
And found my idol,—thee.
Though never love intenser
Had bowed a soul before it,
Thine eye was on the censer,
And not the hand that bore it.

THE PHILOSOPHER TO HIS LOVE

DEAREST, a look is but a ray
Reflected in a certain way;
A word, whatever tone it wear,
Is but a trembling wave of air;
A touch, obedience to a clause
In nature's pure material laws.

The very flowers that bend and meet,
In sweetening others, grow more sweet;
The clouds by day, the stars by night,
Inweave their floating locks of light;
The rainbow, Heaven's own forehead's braid,
Is but the embrace of sun and shade.

Oh! in the hour when I shall feel
Those shadows round my senses steal,
When gentle eyes are weeping o'er
The clay that feels their tears no more,
Then let thy spirit with me be,
Or some sweet angel, likest thee!

How few that love us have we found!
How wide the world that girds them round
Like mountain streams we meet and part,
Each living in the other's heart,
Our course unknown, our hope to be
Yet mingled in the distant sea.

But Ocean coils and heaves in vain,
Bound in the subtle moonbeam's chain;
And love and hope do but obey
Some cold, capricious planet's ray,

Which lights and leads the tide it charms
To Death's dark caves and icy arms.

Alas! one narrow line is drawn,
That links our sunset with our dawn;
In mist and shade life's morning rose,
And clouds are round it at its close;
But ah! no twilight beam ascends
To whisper where that evening ends.

THE POET'S LOT

WHAT is a poet's love? —
To write a girl a sonnet,
To get a ring, or some such thing,
And fustianize upon it.

What is a poet's fame? —
Sad hints about his reason,
And sadder praise from garreteers,
To be returned in season.

Where go the poet's lines? —
Answer, ye evening tapers!
Ye auburn locks, ye golden curls,
Speak from your folded papers!

Child of the ploughshare, smile;
Boy of the counter, grieve not,
Though muses round thy trundle-bed
Their broidered tissue weave not.

The poet's future holds
No civic wreath above him;
Nor slated roof, nor varnished chaise,
Nor wife nor child to love him.

Maid of the village inn,
Who workest woe on satin,
(The grass in black, the graves in green,
The epitaph in Latin,)

Trust not to them who say,
In stanzas, they adore thee;
Oh rather sleep in churchyard clay,
With urn and cherub o'er thee!

TO A BLANK SHEET OF PAPER

WAN-VISAGED thing! thy virgin leaf
To me looks more than deadly pale,
Unknowing what may stain thee yet,—
A poem or a tale.

Who can thy unborn meaning scan?
Can Seer or Sibyl read thee now?
No,—seek to trace the fate of man
Writ on his infant brow.

Love may light on thy snowy cheek,
And shake his Eden-breathing plumes;
Then shalt thou tell how Lelia smiles,
Or Angelina blooms.

Satire may lift his bearded lance,
Forestalling Time's slow-moving scythe,
And, scattered on thy little field,
Disjointed bards may writhe.

Perchance a vision of the night,
Some grizzled spectre, gaunt and thin,
Or sheeted corpse, may stalk along,
Or skeleton may grin.

If it should be in pensive hour
Some sorrow-moving theme I try,
Ah, maiden, how thy tears will fall,
For all I doom to die!

But if in merry mood I touch
Thy leaves, then shall the sight of thee
Sow smiles as thick on rosy lips
As ripples on the sea.

The Weekly press shall gladly stoop
To bind thee up among its sheaves;

The Daily steal thy shining ore,
Tc gild its leaden leaves.

Thou hast no tongue, yet thou canst speak,
Till distant shores shall hear the sound;
Thou hast no life, yet thou canst breathe
Fresh life on all around.

Thou art the arena of the wise,
The noiseless battle-ground of fame;
The sky where halos may be wreathed
Around the humblest name.

Take, then, this treasure to thy trust,
To win some idle reader's smile,
Then fade and moulder in the dust,
Or swell some bonfire's pile.

TO THE PORTRAIT OF "A GENTLEMAN"

IN THE ATHENIEUM GALLERY

IT may be so,—perhaps thou hast
A warm and loving heart;
I will not blame thee for thy face,
Poor devil as thou art.

That thing thou fondly deem'st a nose,
Unsightly though it be,—
In spite of all the cold world's scorn,
It may be much to thee.

Those eyes,—among thine elder friends
Perhaps they pass for blue,—
No matter,—if a man can see,
What more have eyes to do?

Thy mouth,—that fissure in thy face,
By something like a chin,—
May be a very useful place
To put thy victual in.

I know thou hast a wife at home,
I know thou hast a child,
By that subdued, domestic smile
Upon thy features mild.

That wife sits fearless by thy side,
That cherub on thy knee;
They do not shudder at thy looks,
They do not shrink from thee.

Above thy mantel is a hook,—
A portrait once was there;
It was thine only ornament,—
Alas! that hook is bare.

She begged thee not to let it go,
She begged thee all in vain;

She wept,—and breathed a trembling prayer
To meet it safe again.

It was a bitter sight to see
That picture torn away;
It was a solemn thought to think
What all her friends would say!

And often in her calmer hours,
And in her happy dreams,
Upon its long-deserted hook
The absent portrait seems.

Thy wretched infant turns his head
In melancholy wise,
And looks to meet the placid stare
Of those unbending eyes.

I never saw thee, lovely one,—
Perchance I never may;
It is not often that we cross
Such people in our way;

But if we meet in distant years,
Or on some foreign shore,
Sure I can take my Bible oath,
I've seen that face before.

THE BALLAD OF THE OYSTERMAN

IT was a tall young oysterman lived by the river-side,
His shop was just upon the bank, his boat was on the tide;
The daughter of a fisherman, that was so straight and slim,
Lived over on the other bank, right opposite to him.

It was the pensive oysterman that saw a lovely maid,
Upon a moonlight evening, a sitting in the shade;
He saw her wave her handkerchief, as much as if to say,
"I 'm wide awake, young oysterman, and all the folks away."

Then up arose the oysterman, and to himself said he,
"I guess I 'll leave the skiff at home, for fear that folks should see
I read it in the story-book, that, for to kiss his dear,
Leander swam the Hellespont, — and I will swim this here."

And he has leaped into the waves, and crossed the shining stream,
And he has clambered up the bank, all in the moonlight gleam;
Oh there were kisses sweet as dew, and words as soft as rain, —
But they have heard her father's step, and in he leaps again!

Out spoke the ancient fisherman, — "Oh, what was that, my daughter?"
"'T was nothing but a pebble, sir, I threw into the water."
"And what is that, pray tell me, love, that paddles off so fast?"
"It's nothing but a porpoise, sir, that 's been a swimming past."

Out spoke the ancient fisherman, — "Now bring me my harpoon!
I'll get into my fishing-boat, and fix the fellow soon."
Down fell that pretty innocent, as falls a snow-white lamb,
Her hair drooped round her pallid cheeks, like sea-weed on a clam.

Alas for those two loving ones! she waked not from her swound,
And he was taken with the cramp, and in the waves was drowned;
But Fate has metamorphosed them, in pity of their woe,
And now they keep an oyster-shop for mermaids down below.

A NOONTIDE LYRIC

THE dinner-bell, the dinner-bell
Is ringing loud and clear;
Through hill and plain, through street and lane,
It echoes far and near;
From curtained hall and whitewashed stall,
Wherever men can hide,
Like bursting waves from ocean caves,
They float upon the tide.

I smell the smell of roasted meat!
I hear the hissing fry
The beggars know where they can go,
But where, oh where shall I?
At twelve o'clock men took my hand,
At two they only stare,
And eye me with a fearful look,
As if I were a bear!

The poet lays his laurels down,
And hastens to his greens;
The happy tailor quits his goose,
To riot on his beans;
The weary cobbler snaps his thread,
The printer leaves his pi;
His very devil hath a home,
But what, oh what have I?

Methinks I hear an angel voice,
That softly seems to say
"Pale stranger, all may yet be well,
Then wipe thy tears away;
Erect thy head, and cock thy hat,
And follow me afar,
And thou shalt have a jolly meal,
And charge it at the bar."

I hear the voice! I go! I go!
Prepare your meat and wine!
They little heed their future need
Who pay not when they dine.
Give me to-day the rosy bowl,
Give me one golden dream,—
To-morrow kick away the stool,
And dangle from the beam!

THE HOT SEASON

THE folks, that on the first of May
Wore winter coats and hose,
Began to say, the first of June,
"Good Lord! how hot it grows!"
At last two Fahrenheits blew up,
And killed two children small,
And one barometer shot dead
A tutor with its ball!

Now all day long the locusts sang
Among the leafless trees;
Three new hotels warped inside out,
The pumps could only wheeze;
And ripe old wine, that twenty years
Had cobwebbed o'er in vain,
Came spouting through the rotten corks
Like Joly's best champagne.

The Worcester locomotives did
Their trip in half an hour;
The Lowell cars ran forty miles
Before they checked the power;
Roll brimstone soon became a drug,
And loco-focos fell;
All asked for ice, but everywhere
Saltpetre was to sell.

Plump men of mornings ordered tights,
But, ere the scorching noons,
Their candle-moulds had grown as loose
As Cossack pantaloons!
The dogs ran mad,—men could not try
If water they would choose;
A horse fell dead,—he only left
Four red-hot, rusty shoes!

But soon the people could not bear
The slightest hint of fire;
Allusions to caloric drew
A flood of savage ire;

The leaves on heat were all torn out
From every book at school,
And many blackguards kicked and caned,
Because they said, "Keep cool!"

The gas-light companies were mobbed,
The bakers all were shot,
The penny press began to talk
Of lynching Doctor Nott;
And all about the warehouse steps
Were angry men in droves,
Crashing and splintering through the doors
To smash the patent stoves!

The abolition men and maids
Were tanned to such a hue,
You scarce could tell them from their friends,
Unless their eyes were blue;
And, when I left, society
Had burst its ancient guards,
And Brattle Street and Temple Place
Were interchanging cards.

A PORTRAIT

A STILL, sweet, placid, moonlight face,
And slightly nonchalant,
Which seems to claim a middle place
Between one's love and aunt,
Where childhood's star has left a ray
In woman's sunniest sky,
As morning dew and blushing day
On fruit and blossom lie.

And yet,—and yet I cannot love
Those lovely lines on steel;
They beam too much of heaven above,
Earth's darker shades to feel;
Perchance some early weeds of care
Around my heart have grown,
And brows unfurrowed seem not fair,
Because they mock my own.

Alas! when Eden's gates were sealed,
How oft some sheltered flower
Breathed o'er the wanderers of the field,
Like their own bridal bower;
Yet, saddened by its loveliness,
And humbled by its pride,
Earth's fairest child they could not bless,
It mocked them when they sighed.

AN EVENING THOUGHT

WRITTEN AT SEA

IF sometimes in the dark blue eye,
Or in the deep red wine,
Or soothed by gentlest melody,
Still warms this heart of mine,
Yet something colder in the blood,
And calmer in the brain,
Have whispered that my youth's bright flood
Ebbs, not to flow again.

If by Helvetia's azure lake,
Or Arno's yellow stream,
Each star of memory could awake,
As in my first young dream,
I know that when mine eye shall greet
The hillsides bleak and bare,
That gird my home, it will not meet
My childhood's sunsets there.

Oh, when love's first, sweet, stolen kiss
Burned on my boyish brow,
Was that young forehead worn as this?
Was that flushed cheek as now?
Were that wild pulse and throbbing heart
Like these, which vainly strive,
In thankless strains of soulless art,
To dream themselves alive?

Alas! the morning dew is gone,
Gone ere the full of day;
Life's iron fetter still is on,
Its wreaths all torn away;
Happy if still some casual hour
Can warm the fading shrine,
Too soon to chill beyond the power
Of love, or song, or wine!

THE WASP AND THE HORNET

THE two proud sisters of the sea,
In glory and in doom!—
Well may the eternal waters be
Their broad, unsculptured tomb!
The wind that rings along the wave,
The clear, unshadowed sun,
Are torch and trumpet o'er the brave,
Whose last green wreath is won!

No stranger-hand their banners furled,
No victor's shout they heard;
Unseen, above them ocean curled,
Safe by his own pale bird;
The gnashing billows heaved and fell;
Wild shrieked the midnight gale;
Far, far beneath the morning swell
Were pennon, spar, and sail.

The land of Freedom! Sea and shore
Are guarded now, as when
Her ebbing waves to victory bore
Fair barks and gallant men;
Oh, many a ship of prouder name
May wave her starry fold,
Nor trail, with deeper light of fame,
The paths they swept of old!

"QUI VIVE?"

"Qui vive?" The sentry's musket rings,
The channelled bayonet gleams;
High o'er him, like a raven's wings
The broad tricolored banner flings
Its shadow, rustling as it swings
Pale in the moonlight beams;
Pass on! while steel-clad sentries keep
Their vigil o'er the monarch's sleep,
Thy bare, unguarded breast
Asks not the unbroken, bristling zone
That girds yon sceptred trembler's throne;—
Pass on, and take thy rest!

"Qui vive?" How oft the midnight air
That startling cry has borne!
How oft the evening breeze has fanned
The banner of this haughty land,
O'er mountain snow and desert sand,
Ere yet its folds were torn!
Through Jena's carnage flying red,
Or tossing o'er Marengo's dead,
Or curling on the towers
Where Austria's eagle quivers yet,
And suns the ruffled plumage, wet
With battle's crimson showers!

"Qui vive?" And is the sentry's cry,—
The sleepless soldier's hand,—
Are these—the painted folds that fly
And lift their emblems, printed high
On morning mist and sunset sky—
The guardians of a land?
No! If the patriot's pulses sleep,
How vain the watch that hirelings keep,
The idle flag that waves,
When Conquest, with his iron heel,
Treads down the standards and the steel
That belt the soil of slaves!